GUJARATI SELF-TAUGHT

BY THE NATURAL METHOD WITH PHONETIC PRONUNCIATION (THIMM'S SYSTEM)

GUJARATI SELF-TAUGHT

BY THE NATURAL METHOD WITH PHONETIC PRONUNCIATION (THIMM'S SYSTEM)

N. M. DHRUVA

GYAN

Published by

Gyan Publishing House
5, Ansari Road
Daryaganj, New Delhi-110002
Phone: 011-47034999, 9811692060
E-mail: books@gyanbooks.com

Distribution Network
gyanbooks.com
India, USA, Canada, UK, Australia, France

ISBN : 978-81-212-3451-1 (PB)
First Published, 1920

2nd Impression 2020

Printed at: Gyan Press, Delhi.

Gujarati Self-Taught
Author: N. M. Dhruva

Marlborough Self Taught Series

Gujarati Self-Taught

by the Natural Method.

WITH

Phonetic Pronunciation.

THIMM'S SYSTEM.

BY

N. M. DHRUVA.

Grasia College, Gondal (Kathiawar, India.)

Printed in Great Britain.

LONDON:

E. MARLBOROUGH & CO LTD., 51 & 52 OLD BAILEY, E.C.4.

PREFACE.

THIS volume of Gujarati is primarily intended to supply a working and practical knowledge of the language for the benefit of those who require to use the spoken tongue for the purposes of business or pleasure. With this in view many vocabularies are supplied carefully selected to suit the needs of the Gujarati speaking districts and classified according to subject, and also a large number of colloquial phrases and sentences of a practical character, similarly classified. Throughout the volume the pronunciation of the Gujarati words is added, according to Marlborough's system of phonetics—a system which has grown out of long experience, and is of so simple a nature that, by means of it, a stranger to the language who knows English only, can read off the words at a glance and thus easily make himself understood amongst Gujarati speaking people. At the same time the main principles and the most important rules of the Grammar of Gujrati are supplied, with vocabularies and exercises, thus enabling the student to obtain an intelligent acquaintance with the structure of the language, and to pave the way to a thorough knowledge of it later on.

GRASIA COLLEGE,
Gondal. (Kathiawar-India.)
July 1920.

N. M. DHRUVA.

CONTENTS.

I. THE ALPHABET AND PRONUNCIATION—Pages 1 to 5.
Consonants 1
Consonants and Vowel signs combined 3
Preliminary Notes 5
Vowel Letters 1
Vowel Letters and signs 3
II. VOCABULARIES—Pages 6 to 60.
Adjectives 47
Adverbs, Conjunctions and Prepositions 57
Animals, Birds and Insects 10
Cardinal Numbers 42
Commercial Terms 31
Diseases, Drugs, &c. 20
Dress and the Toilet 23
Food 22
House and Household Articles 25
Human Body 19
Legal and Trading Terms 34
Mankind: Relations 17
Metals, Minerals and Jewels 8
Miscellaneous Words 40
Ordinal Numbers 46
Professions and Trades 28
Pronouns 46
Religious Terms 38
Shooting and Fishing 37
Time and Seasons &c. 14
Days of the Week 16
Hindu Months 16
Muhammedan Months 17
Parsi Months 17
Seasons 16
Travelling 27
Trees, Fruits, Flowers and Vegetables 12

Verbs 50
World and Nature 6
III. Outline of Grammar—Pages 61 to 81.
Adjectives 66
Arrangement of words in a Sentence 61
Can, May, Must, Should, ought to 79
Case 63
Future Tense 76
Gender 62
Have, to 70
Number 63
Past Tense 71
Past Imperfect Tense 75
Personal Pronouns 64
Pluperfect Tense 77
Present Tense 68
Present Tense of "to be".. 67
Present Perfect Tense 77
Was, Had 73
IV. Conversational Phrases and Sentences—Pages 82 to 108
Breakfast, Tea, Dinner &c. 94
Correspondence 100
Domestic Servants 101
Fishing 104
Greetings and Polite Expressions 82
Idiomatic Expressions 89
In Town 95
Shooting 105
Shopping 97
Study of Gujarati 83
Time and weather 107
Travelling by Railway 92
Useful and Necessary Expressions 84
V. Exercises for Translation— Pages 109 to 112
VI. Money and Weights 113

GUJARATI SELF-TAUGHT.

I The Alphabet and Pronunciation.

The Vowel Letters.

Letters.	Roman character	Pronunciation.
અ	*u*	as *u* in *up, furrow.*
આ	*ā*	,, *a* ,, *far.*
ઇ	*i*	,, *i* ,, *bit.*
ઈ	*ee*	,, *ee* ,, *steel.*
ઉ	*ŏŏ*	,, *oo* ,, *foot.*
ઊ	*oo*	,, *oo* ,, *moon.*
એ	*e*	,, *e* ,, *bet.*
ઐ	*ai*	,, *ai* ,, *bait.*
ઓ	*o*	,, *o* ,, *tone.*
ઔ	*ow*	,, *ow* ,, *town.*
અં	*ṅ*	soft nasal as in *lung.*
અઃ	*uh*	generally not used.

The Consonants.

Letters.	Roman character	Pronunciation.
ક	*k*	as in *king.*
ખ	*kh*	guttural as in *loch.*
ગ	*g*	as in *gun.*
ઘ	*gh*	*g* with aspirate sounded together (*g*+*h*)
ચ	*ch*	as in *church.*
છ	*ch*	*ch* with aspirate sounded together (*ch*+*h*)
જ	*j*	as in *judge*
ઝ	*jh*	*j* with aspirate sounded together (*j*+*h*)
ટ	*t*	as *t* in *table.*
ઠ	*th*	*t* with aspirate sounded together (*t*+*h*)
ડ	*ḍ*	as *d* in *dull.*
ઢ	*dh*	*ḍ* with aspirate sounded together (*d*+*h*).

Letters.	Roman character	Pronunciation.
ણ	*ṇ*	nearly as the nasal sound heard in *Colonel.*
ત	*t*	uttered with point of tongue on roots of upper teeth.
થ	*th*	as in *thin.*
દ	*d*	uttered with point of tongue on roots of upper teeth.
ધ	*dh*	*d* with aspiration sounded together (*d*+*h*)
ન	*n*	as in *nun.*
પ	*p*	as in *pain.*
ફ	*f*	,, *fame.*
બ	*b*	,, *baby.*
ભ	*bh*	*b* with aspiration sounded together (*b*+*h*)
મ	*m*	as in *mug*
ય	*y*	,, *yarn.*
ર	*r*	,, *run.*
લ	*l*	,, *luck.*
વ	*v*	,, *vain.*
શ	*sh*	,, *shine.*
ષ	*sh*	*s* with aspiration sounded together (*s*+*h*)
સ	*s*	as in *sin* (always sharp)
હ	*h*	,, *hum.*
ળ	*ḷ*	*l* sound uttered with the tip of the tongue curved backward.
ક્ષ	*ksh*	as *ctio* in fraction.
જ્ઞ	*gn*	,, *agnate.*

The Vowels.

There are two ways of writing the vowels:—

(1) The whole vowel is written when used by itself (*i. e.* independently of the consonant) in the formation of a word as, અરબ, urub, *an Arab.*

(2) When vowels are combined with consonants, they are not written in full, but vowel signs only are used, as follows:—

Vowel letters.	Vowel signs.	Joined to a consonant.	Pronunciation.
અ	(none)	ક	*ku* as *cu* in cut.
આ	ા	કા	*kā* as *ca* in car.
ઇ	િ	કિ	*ki* as in kit.
ઈ	ી	કી	*kee* ,, keel.
ઉ	ુ	કુ	*kŏŏ* as *cou* in could.
ઊ	ૂ	કૂ	*koo* as *coo* in cool.
એ	ે	કે	*ke* as in kettle.
ઐ	ૈ	કૈ	*kai* ,, kail.
ઓ	ો	કો	*ko* ,, kodak.
ઔ	ૌ	કૌ	*kow* like cow.
અં	ં	કં	*kn* soft nasal as in ung.
અઃ	ઃ	કઃ	*kuh* (not used).

Consonants and Vowel Signs combined.

Consonant and Vowel letters	Consonant and Vowel Signs.	Pronunciation.	Examples.
ક + અ	ક	*ku*	કલમ, *kulum*, a pen.
ક + આ	કા	*kā*	કામ, *kām*, work.
ક + ઇ	કિ	*ki*	કિડિ, *kiḍi*, an ant.
ક + ઈ	કી	*kee*	કીમત, *keemut*, price.
ક + ઉ	કુ	*kŏŏ*	કુકડી, *kŏŏkḍee*, a hen.
ક + ઊ	કૂ	*koo*	કૂચ, *kooch*, march.
ક + એ	કે	*ke*	કેદી, *kedee*, a prisoner.

Consonant and Vowel lette.s.	C..nsonant and Vowel Signs.	Pronun-ciation.	Examples.
ક+ઐ	કૈ	*kai*	કૈલાસ, *kailās*, para lise.
ક+ઓ	કો	*ko*	કોટડી, *kotdee*, a room.
ક+ઔ	કૌ	*kow*	કૌવત, *kowvut*, strength.
ક+અં	કં	*kung*	કંગાલ, *kungāl*, a beggar.
ક+અઃ	કઃ	*kuh*	(not used)

Note.—The combination of the consonant જ (j) with the vowels ઈ, ઉ, and ઊ is peculiar and may therefore be noted:—જ+ઈ=જી=*jee*; જ+ઉ=જુ=*jŏŏ*; and જ+ઊ=જૂ=*joo*.

All other consonants are combined with the vowel—signs as shewn in the above table; as, લ+ઈ=લી• *lee*; &c

Preliminary Notes.

When a consonant is pronounced, it is necessary to add a vowel in order to give it a full and distinct sound. Thus all Gujarati Consonants have the sound of U inherent in them; but as a rule the final consonant in a word is pronounced without the U; as *kulum*.

The following four points of advantage possessed by Gujarati orthography make it easy to acquire a correct knowledge of pronunciation and spelling:—

1. Each sound is represented by a distinct letter, and that one sound is always the same.
2. No sound is represented by more than one letter.
3. A word has no redundant letters in it.
4. It is very concise, as the Vowels and the nasals are not written in their full forms, but are represented by signs only

Conjunct Letters.

Those consonants that have the perpendicular stroke, drop the stroke, and to the remnant is affixed the letter following, as બ+દ=બ્દ bd. In the case of other letters, the usual method of combining them is to write the combining letters side by side in contact, as ક+ત=ક્ત kt.

The combination of જ with ી, ુ, ૂ and of ર with ુ is peculiar and may therefore be noted, as જી, જુ, જૂ and રુ.

The mode of combining ર is different in different places. When it precedes a consonant with which it is to be combined, it is written like ^ above that consonant; as પૂર્વ purv; when it follows a consonant it is written like / by side of the preceding consonant with a perpendicular stroke; as પ્ર pr, and underneath like ^ with letters without perpendicular strokes; as ટ્ર tr.

The sign ‸ represents શ when combined with ન, ર, લ, વ as શ્ન, શ્ર, શ્લ, શ્વ.

The combination of દ+મ=દ્મ; દ+ય=દ્ય, શ+ર=શ્ર; હ+ય=હ્ય and હ+મ=હ્મ should also be noted.

II.—Vocabularies.

The world and Nature.

English	Gujarati	Gujarati (romanized)
Air	હવા *f.*	*huvā*
bay	ઉપસાગર *m.*	*oŏpsāgur*
channel	ખાડી *f.*	*khāḍee*
climate	હવા-પાણી *n. p.*	*huvā-pāṇee*
clouds	વાદળાં *n. p.*	*vādḷāṅ*
coast	કાંઠો, કિનારો *m.*	*kānṭho, kinār*
cold	ટાઢ, ઠંડી *f:*	*ṭāḍh, ṭhuṅḍe*
comet	ધૂમકેતુ *m.*	*dhoomketoŏ*
continent	ખંડ *m.*	*khuṇḍ*
country	દેશ *m.*	*desh*
darkness	અંધારૂં *n*	*uṅdhārŏŏṅ*
desert	રણ *n.*	*ruṇ*
dew	ઝાકળ *f.*	*jhākuḷ*
dust	ધૂળ, માટી *f.*	*dhooḷ, māṭee*
earth	પૃથ્વી *f.*	*pruthvee*
—quake	ધરતીકંપ *m.*	*dhurtee-kuṅp*
east	પૂર્વ *f.*	*poorv*
ebb	ઓટ *f.*	*oṭ*
eclipse	ગ્રહણ *n.*	*gruhuṇ*
fire	આગ, અગ્નિ *f. m.*	*āg, ugni*
flood	રેલ, ભરતી *f.*	*rel, bhurtee*
foam	ફીણ *n.*	*feeṇ*
fog	ધુમસ *f. m.*	*dhŏŏmus*
frost	હિમ *n.*	*him*
full-moon	પૂંનમ *f.*	*poonum*
geography	ભૂગોળ *f.*	*bhoogoḷ*
gulf	અખાત *m.*	*ukhāt*
hails	કરા *m. p*	*kurā*
heaven, paradise	સ્વર્ગ *n.*	*svurg*

English	Gujarati	Gujarati (romanized)
heat	તાપ, ગરમી *m. f.*	*tāp, gurmee*
hell	નર્ક *n.*	*nurk*
hill	ટેકરી *f.*	*ṭekree*
island	બેટ *m.*	*beṭ*
lake	સરોવર *n.*	*surovur*
land	જમીન *f.*	*jumeen*
light	અજવાળું *n.*	*ujvāḷoo̐n*
lightning	વિજળી *f.*	*vijḷee*
mainland	ખંડ *m.*	*khunḍ*
mist	ધુમસ *m.*	*dhoo̐mus*
moon	ચંદ્ર *m.*	*chundr*
moonlight	ચાંદની *f.*	*chāndnee*
mountain	પર્વત *m.*	*purvut*
mud	કાદવ *m.*	*kāduv*
nature	કુદરત *f.*	*koo̐drut*
north	ઉત્તર *f.*	*oo̐ttur*
ocean	મહાસાગર *m.*	*muhā-sāgur*
peninsula	દ્વીપકલ્પ *m.*	*dveep-kulp*
plain	મેદાન *n.*	*medān*
planet	ગ્રહ *m.*	*gruh*
polar-star	ધ્રુવ-તારો *m.*	*dhroo̐v-tāro*
pond, tank	તળાવ *n.*	*tuḷav*
rain	વરસાદ *m.*	*vursād*
rainbow	મેઘ-ધનુષ્ય *n.*	*megh-dhunoo̐shy*
rays	કિરણ *n. p.*	*kiruṇ*
river	નદી *f.*	*nudee*
rivulet	નાળું *n.*	*nāḷoo̐n*
rock	ખડક *f.*	*khuḍuk*
sand	રેતી *f.*	*retee*
sea	સમુદ્ર, દરીયો *m.*	*sumoo̐dr, duriyo*
seaport	બંદર *n.*	*bundur*
seashore	દરિયા-કાંઠો *m*	*duriyā-kānṭh*

English	Gujarati	Gujarati (romanized)
shade, shadow	છાયો *m.*	*c<u>h</u>āyo*
sky	આકાશ *n.*	*ākāsh*
snow, ice	બરફ *n.*	*buruf*
south	દક્ષિણ *f.*	*duk<u>sh</u>iṇ*
stars	તારા *m. p.*	*tārā*
storm	તોફાન *n.*	*tofān*
stream	ઝરો *m.*	*j<u>h</u>uro*
sun	સૂર્ય, સુરજ *m.*	*soory, sŏŏruj*
tide	ભરતી *f.*	*<u>bh</u>urtee*
thunder	ગર્જના *f.*	*gurjunā*
town	શહેર, ગામ *n.*	*shuher, gām*
valley	ખીણ *f.*	*<u>kh</u>eeṇ*
village	ગામડું *n.*	*gāmḍŏŏn*
waterfall	ધોધ *m.*	*dhodh*
waves	મોજાં *n. p.*	*mojān*
weather	હવા *f.*	*huvā*
well	કૂવો *m.*	*koovo*
west	પશ્ચિમ *f.*	*pushchim*
whirl-wind	વંટોળિયો *m.*	*vuntoliyo*
wind	પવન, વા *m.*	*puwun, vā*
world	જગત, દુનિયા *n. f.*	*jugut, dŏŏniyā*

Metals, Minerals and Jewels.

Agate	અકીક *n.*	*ukeek*
alum	ફટકડી *f.*	*futukḍee*
bangle	બંગડી *f.*	*bungḍee*
brass	પિતળ *n.*	*pituḷ*
brooch	લોલક *n*	*loluk*
chain	સાંકળી, છેડો *f. m.*	*sānkḷee, c<u>h</u>eḍo*
chalk	ચાક *m.*	*chāk*
clay	માટી *f.*	*māṭee*
coal	કોલસો *m.*	*kolso*

English	Gujarati	Gujarati (romanized)
copper	ત્રાંબુ *n.*	*trānbŏŏ*
coral	પરવાળાં *n. p.*	*purvāḷān*
diamond	હીરો *m.*	*heero*
ear-ring	એરિંગ *n.*	*ering*
emerald	જમરૂદ, પાનું *n:*	*jumrŏŏd, pānŏŏn*
flint	ચકમક *m.*	*chukmuk*
gold	સોનું *n.*	*sonŏŏn*
gravel	કાંકરી *f.*	*kānkree*
iron	લોઢું *n.*	*lodhŏŏn*
jewel	રત્ન *n.*	*rutn*
lead	સિસું *n.*	*sisŏŏn*
lime	ચુનો *m.*	*chŏŏno*
marble	આરસ *m.*	*ārus*
mercury	પારો *m.*	*pāro*
metal	ધાતુ *f.*	*dhātŏŏ*
mineral	ખનિજ *n.*	*khunij*
necklace	કંઠી *f.*	*kunṭhee*
pearl	મોતી *n.*	*motee*
ring	વીંટી *f.*	*veenṭee*
ruby	માણેક *n.*	*māṇek*
sapphire	નીલમ *n.*	*neelum*
silver	રૂપું, ચાંદી *n. f.*	*rŏŏpŏŏn, chāndee*
soda (carbonate of)	ખારો *m.*	*khāro*
steel	પોલાદ, ગજવેલ *n. f.*	*polād, gujvel*
stone	પત્થર *m.*	*put-thur*
tin	કલઇ *f.*	*k·lui*
topaz	પોખરાજ *n.*	*pokhrāj*
zinc	જસત *n.*	*jusut*

Animals, Birds and Insects.

English	Gujarati	Gujarati (romanized)
Alligator	મગર *m.*	*mugur*
ant	કિડી *f.*	*kiḍee*
ass, donkey	ગધેડો *m.*	*gudheḍo*
bear	રીંછ *n.*	*reeinch*
beast	પશુ *n.*	*pusho͝o*
bird	પક્ષી *n.*	*pukshee*
buck	કાળિયાર *m.*	*kāḷiyār*
buffalo	ભેંસ *f.*	*bhens*
bugs	માંકડ *m. p.*	*mānkuḍ*
bullock, ox	બળદ *m*	*buḷud*
butterfly	પતંગિયું *n.*	*putungiyo͝on*
camel	ઊંટ *m.*	*ooṅṭ*
cat	બિલાડી *f.*	*bilāḍee*
cow	ગાય *f.*	*gāy*
crane	બગલો *m.*	*buglo*
crow	કાગડો *m.*	*kāgḍo*
cuckoo	કોયલ *f.*	*koyul*
dog	કૂતરો *m.*	*kootro*
duck	બતક *f.*	*butuk*
eagle	ગરૂડ *m.*	*guro͝oḍ*
elephant	હાથી *m.*	*hāthee*
falcon, hawk	બાજ *m.*	*bāj*
flea	ચાંચડ *m.*	*chānchuḍ*
fly	માખી *f*	*mākhee*
fox	લોંકડી *f*	*loṅkḍee*
frogs	દેડકાં *n. p.*	*deḍkāṅ*
goat	બકરો *m.*	*bukro*
hare, rabbit	સસલું *n.*	*suslo͝oṅ*
horse	ઘોડો *m.*	*ghoḍo*
jackal	શિયાળ *n.*	*shiyāḷ*

English	Gujarati	Gujarati (romanized)
kite	સમડી *f.*	*sumḍee*
lamb, sheep	ઘેટું *n.*	*gheṭo͝on*
leopard	ચિત્તો *m.*	*chitto*
lion	સિંહ *m.*	*siṅh*
lizzard	ગરોળી *f.*	*guroḷee*
locust	તીડ *n.*	*teeḍ*
monkey	વાંદરો *m.*	*vāṅdro*
mosquito	મચ્છર *n.*	*much-chur*
mouse, rat	ઉંદર *m.*	*o͝oṅdur*
mule	ખચર *n.*	*khuchur*
owl	ઘુવડ *n.*	*gho͝ovuḍ*
panther	દીપડો *m.*	*deepḍo*
parrot	પોપટ *m.*	*popuṭ*
peacock	મોર *m.*	*mor*
pig	ડુક્કર *n.*	*ḍo͝okkur*
pigeon, dove	કબુતર *n.*	*kubo͝otur*
pony	ટટ્ટુ *n.*	*ṭuṭṭo͝o*
poultry	મુરઘાં *n. p.*	*mo͝orghāṅ*
rhinoceros	ગેંડું *n.*	*geṅḍo͝oṅ*
scorpion	વીંછી *m.*	*veeṅchhee*
snake	સાપ *m.*	*sāp*
sparrow	ચકલી *f.*	*chuklee*
spider	કરોળિયો *m.*	*kuroḷiyo*
squirrel	ખિસકોલી *f.*	*khiskolee*
stag	સાબર *n.*	*sābur*
tiger	વાઘ *m.*	*vāgh*
tortoise	કાચબો *m.*	*kāchbo*
vulture	ગીધ *n.*	*geedh*
wasp, hornet	ભમરો *m.*	*bhumro*
weasel	નોળિયું *n.*	*noḷiyo͝oṅ*
white-ant	ઉધાઇ *f.*	*o͝odhāi*
wolf	વરુ *n.*	*vuro͝o*

Trees, Fruits, Flowers and Vegetables.

English	Gujarati	Gujarati (romanized)
Almond	બદામ *f.*	*budām*
apple	સફરજન *n.*	*sufurjun*
babul-tree	બાવળ *m.*	*bāvuḷ*
bamboo	વાંસ *m.*	*vāns*
bananas	સોનેરી કેળાં *n. p.*	*soneree keḷān*
black-wood	સીસમ *n.*	*seesum*
boquet	ગજરેા *m.*	*gujro*
brinjals	રિંગણું *n. p.*	*ringṇān*
bud	કુળી *f.*	*kuḷee*
cabbage	કેાબી *n.*	*kobee*
cactus	થેાર *m.*	*thor*
carrots	ગાજર *n. p.*	*gājur*
chilli	મરચાં *n. p.*	*murchān*
cocoanut	નાળિયેર *n.*	*nāḷiyer*
creeper	વેલેા *m.*	*velo*
cucumber	કાકડી *f.*	*kākḍee*
custard-apple	સીતાફળ *n.*	*seetāfuḷ*
date	ખજુર, ખારેક *f.*	*khujŏŏr*, *khārek*
ebony	અબનુસ *n.*	*ubnŏŏs*
figs	અંજીર *n. p*	*unjeer*
flower	ફુલ *n.*	*fŏŏl*
fruit	ફળ *n.*	*fuḷ*
garland	હાર *m.*	*hār*
garlic	લસણ *n.*	*lusuṇ*
gourd	દૂધી *f.*	*doodhee*
grapes	દ્રાક્ષ *f.*	*drāksh*
guava	જામફળ *n.*	*jāmfuḷ*
hemp	શણ *n.*	*shuṇ*
jack-fruit	ફણસ *n*	*funus*
jasmine	જુઇ *f.*	*jŏŏ-i*

English	Gujarati	Gujarati (romanized)
jessamine	ચમેલી *f*	*chumelee*
jujube-tree	બોરડી *f.*	*borḍee*
lemon	લીંબુ *n.*	*leeṅbŏŏ*
lotus	કમળ *n.*	*kumuḷ*
maize	મકાઇ *f.*	*mukāi*
mango	કેરી *f.*	*keree*
mango-tree	આંબો *m.*	*āṅbo*
mint	ફુદીનો *m.*	*fŏŏdeeno*
mulberry	શેતુર *n.*	*shetŏŏr*
onion	ડુંગળી, કાંદા *f*	*ḍŏŏṅglee, kāṅdā*
orange	નારંગી *f.*	*nāruṅgee*
palm-tree	તાડ *m.*	*tāḍ*
pine-apple	અનેનાસ *n.*	*unenās*
plantains	કેળાં *n. p*	*keḷāṅ*
plantain-tree	કેળ *f.*	*keḷ*
pomegranate	દાડમ *n.*	*dāḍum*
potatoes	બટાટાં *n. p.*	*buṭāṭāṅ*
pumpkin	કોળું *n.*	*koḷŏŏṅ*
radish	મૂળો *m.*	*mooḷo*
rose	ગુલાબ *m*	*gŏŏlāb*
sandal-wood	સુખડ *f.*	*sŏŏkhuḍ*
sugar-cane	શેરડી *f*	*sherḍee*
tamarind	આંબલી *f.*	*āṅblee*
teak-wood	સાગ *m.*	*sāg*
tree	ઝાડ *n.*	*jhāḍ*
vegetables	શાક-ભાજી *f.*	*shāk-bhājee*
walnut	અખોડ *n.*	*ukhoḍ*
water-melon	તરબુચ *n.*	*turbŏŏch*

Time and Seasons &c.

English	Gujarati	Gujarati (romanized)
Afternoon	બપોર પછી	*bupor-puchee*
beginning	શરૂ	*shrŏŏ*
birthday	વર્ષગાંઠ *f.*	*vurshgānth*
christmas	નાતાળ	*nātāḷ*
dawn	પ્રભાત *n.*	*prubhāt*
day	દિવસ *m.*	*divus*
day and a half	દોઢ દિવસ *m.*	*dodh divus*
day by day	દિવસોદિવસ	*divus-o-divus*
day of the month	તારીખ *f.*	*tāreekh*
——week	વાર *m*	*vār*
day after to-morrow day before yesterday	પરમ દિવસ *m.*	*purum-divus*
daybreak	પરોઢિયું *n.*	*purodhiyŏŏn*
every day	દરરોજ	*dur-roj*
from day to day	રોજેરોજનું	*roje-rojnŏŏn*
in a few days	થોડા દિવસમાં	*thoḍā divus-mān*
some days ago	થોડા દિવસ પહેલાં	*thoḍā divus puhelān*
easter	ઇસ્ટર (*E*)	*istur*
end	આખર *f.*	*ākhur*
evening	સાંજ *f.*	*sānj*
fortnight	પખવાડિયું *n.*	*pukhvāḍiyŏŏn*
holiday	તહેવાર *m.*	*tuhevār*
hour	કલાક *m.*	*kulāk*
—, half an	અરધો કલાક *m.*	*urdho kulāk*
—, quarter of an	પા કલાક *m.*	*pā kulāk*
hourly	કલાકે કલાકે	*kulāke kulāke*
last night	ગઇરાતે *f.*	*gui rāte*
later	મોડેથી	*moḍethee*

English	Gujarati	Gujarati (romanized)
mid-day	મધ્યાન, બપોર *m.*	*mudhyān, bupor*
midnight	મધરાત *f.*	*mudh-rāt*
midsummer	ખરો ઉનાળો *m.*	*k͟huro ŏŏnāḷo*
month	મહિનો, માસ *m.*	*muhino, mās*
—last	ગયે મહિને	*guye muhine*
—next	આવતે મહિને	*āvute muhine*
monthly	માસિક	*māsik*
morning	સવાર *f.*	*suvār*
night	રાત *f.*	*rāt*
nightly	રોજ રાતે	*roj rāte*
noon	મધ્યાન, બપોર *m.*	*mudhyān, bupor*
now	હમણાં	*humṇān*
now-a-days	આજકાલ	*ājkāl*
part	ભાગ *m.*	*b͟hāg*
quarter	પા ભાગ *m.*	*pā-b͟hāg*
season	રૂતુ *f.*	*rŏŏtŏŏ*
second	પળ *f.*	*puḷ*
sunrise	સૂર્યોદય *m.*	*sooryoduy*
sunset	સૂર્યાસ્ત *m.*	*sooryāst*
time	વખત *m.*	*vuk͟hut*
today	આજ *f.*	*āj*
tomorrow	આવતી કાલ *f.*	*āvtee kāl*
—morning	કાલ સવારે	*kāl suvāre*
tonight	આજ રાતે	*āj rāte*
twilight	સંધ્યા *f.*	*sundhyā*
week	અઠવાડિયું *n.*	*ut͟hvāḍiyŏŏn*
weekly	અઠવાડિયે	*ut͟hvāḍiye*
whole	આખું *n.*	*āk͟hŏŏn*
year	વર્ષ *n.*	*vurs͟h*
yearly	વાર્ષિક	*vārs͟hik*
yesterday	ગઇ કાલ *f.*	*gui-kāl*
—morning	ગઇ કાલ સવારે	*gui kāl suvāre*
—night	ગઇ કાલ રાતે	*gui kāl rāte*

The Days of the Week

English	Gujarati	Gujarati (romanized)
Sunday	રવિવાર *m.*	*ruvivār*
Monday	સોમવાર *m.*	*somvār*
Tuesday	મંગળવાર *m.*	*muṅguḷvār*
Wednesday	બુધવાર *m.*	*bo͝odhvār*
Thursday	ગુરૂવાર *m.*	*go͝oro͝ovār*
Friday	શુક્રવાર *m.*	*sho͝okrvār*
Saturday	શનિવાર *m.*	*shunivār*

The Months.

English	Gujarati	Gujarati (romanized)
November	કાર્તિક *m*	*kārtuk*
December	માગશર *m.*	*māgshur*
January	પોષ *m.*	*posh*
February	માહા *m.*	*māhā*
March	ફાગણ *m.*	*fāguṇ*
April	ચૈતર *m.*	*chaitur*
May	વૈશાખ *m.*	*vaishākh*
June	જેઠ *m.*	*jeth*
July	આષાઢ *m.*	*āshādh*
August	શ્રાવણ *m.*	*shrāvuṇ*
September	ભાદરવો *m.*	*bhādurvo*
October	આશો *m.*	*āsho*

The Seasons

English	Gujarati	Gujarati (romanized)
Winter	શિયાળો *m.*	*shiyāḷo*
Spring	વસંત *f.*	*vusunt*
Autumn	પાનખર *f.*	*pānkhur*
Summer	ઉનાળો *m.*	*o͝onāḷo*
Rainy season	ચોમાસું *n.*	*chomāso͝on*

The Muhammedan Months.

Name of month in Gujarati.	Gujarati (romanized).
મોહરમ	*mohurum*
સફર	*sufur*
રબિ-ઉલ-અવ્વલ	*rubi-ŏol-uvvul*
રબિ-ઉલ-આખર	*rubi-ŏol-ākhur*
જમાદિ-ઉલ-અવ્વલ	*jumādi-ŏol-uvvul*
જમાદિ-ઉલ-આખર	*jumādi-ŏol-ākhur*
રજબ	*rujub*
શાબાન	*shu-u-bān*
રમઝાન	*rumjhān*
શવ્વાલ	*shuvvāl*
જિલકદ	*jhilkud*
જિલહજ	*jhilhuj*

The Parsi Months.

ફરવરદીન	*furvurdeen*
અરદીબેહિશ્ત	*urdee-behisht*
ખોરદાદ	*khordād*
તીર	*teer*
અમરદાદ	*umurdād*
શહેરેવર	*shuherevur*
મેહર	*mehur*
આવાં	*āvān*
આદર	*ādur*
દે	*ae*
બહમન	*buhmun*
અસફંદાર	*usfundār*

Mankind: Relations.

English	Gujarati	Gujarati (romanized)
Ancestors	બાપદાદા *m. p.*	*bāp-dāda*
aunt (paternal)	ફોઇ *f.*	*foi*
(maternal)	માશી *f.*	*māsee*

English	Gujarati	Gujarati (romanized)
brother	ભાઇ *m.*	*bhāi*
brother's daughter	ભત્રિજી *f.*	*bhutrijee*
,, son	ભત્રિજો *m.*	*bhutrijo*
child	છોકરૂં, બાળક *n.*	*chokroon, bāḷuk*
cousin	પિતરાઇ *m. or f.*	*pitrāi*
daughter	દીકરી *f.*	*deekree*
family	કુટુંબ *n.*	*kootoonb*
father	બાપ *m.*	*bāp*
father-in-law	સસરો *m.*	*susro*
girl	છોકરી *f.*	*chokree*
grandfather	દાદો *m.*	*dādo*
grandmother	દાદી *f.*	*dādee*
grandson	પૌત્ર *m.*	*powtr*
heir	વારસ *m. or f.*	*vārus*
husband	ધણી *m.*	*dhuṇee*
husband's sister	નણંદ *f.*	*nuṇund*
man	આદમી *m.*	*ādmee*
marriage	લગ્ન *n.*	*lugn*
mother	મા *f.*	*mā*
mother-in-law	સાસુ *f.*	*sāsoo*
nephew	ભાણેજ, ભત્રિજો *m.*	*bhāṇej, bhutrijo*
parents	માબાપ	*mā-bāp*
sister	બહેન *f.*	*buhen*
sister's son	ભાણેજ *m.*	*bhāṇej*
,, daughter	ભાણેજ *f.*	*bhāṇej*
,, husband	બનેવી *m.*	*bunevee*
son	દીકરો *m.*	*deekro*
uncle (paternal)	કાકો *m*	*kāko*
uncle's wife	કાકી *f.*	*kākee*
uncle (maternal)	મામો *m.*	*māmo*
uncle's wife	મામી *f.*	*māmee*
wife	વહુ, સ્ત્રી *f.*	*vuhoo, stree*

English	Gujarati	Gujarati (romanized)
wife's brother	સાળો *m.*	*sāḷo*
,, sister	સાળી *f.*	*sāḷee*

The Human Body.

Back	પીઠ *f.*	*peeṭh*
beard	દાઢી *f.*	*dāḍhee*
belly, stomach	પેટ *n.*	*peṭ*
blood	લોહી *n.*	*lohee*
body	શરીર *n.*	*shureer*
bones	હાડકાં *n. p.*	*hāḍkāṅ*
cheeks	ગાલ *m. p.*	*gāl*
chest	છાતી *f.*	*chātee*
ears	કાન *m p.*	*kān*
elbow	કોણી *f.*	*koṇee*
eyes	આંખો *f. p.*	*āṅkho*
feet	પગ *m. p.*	*pug*
finger	આંગળી *f.*	*āṅguḷee*
forehead	કપાળ *n.*	*kupāḷ*
hair	વાળ *m. p.*	*vāḷ*
hand, arm	હાથ *m.*	*hāth*
head	માથું *n*	*māthŏŏṅ*
heart	હૃદય *n.*	*hruduy*
jaw	જડબું *n.*	*juḍbŏŏṅ*
joints	સાંધા *m. p.*	*sāṅdhā*
knee	ઘુંટણ *n.*	*ghŏŏṅṭuṇ*
lips	હોઠ *m. p.*	*hoṭh*
lung	ફેફસું *n.*	*fefsŏŏṅ*
mouth	મોઢું, મ્હોં *n.*	*moḍhŏṅ, mhoṅ*
nails	નખ *m. p.*	*nukh*
neck	ગરદન *f.*	*gurdun*
nose	નાક *n.*	*nāk*
nostrils	નસકોરાં *n. p.*	*nuskoṛāṅ*

Travelling.

English	Gujarati	Gujarati (romanized)
Arrival	આગમન *n.*	*āgumun*
bag	થેલો *m.*	*thelo*
bill	હિસાબ *m.*	*hisāb*
bridle, reins	લગામ *f.*	*lugām*
box, trunk	પેટી *f.*	*peṭee*
camp	છાવણી *f.*	*c̱ẖāvuṇee*
carriage	ગાડી *f.*	*gāḍee*
coachman	ગાડીવાળો *m.*	*gāḍee-vāḷo*
cushion	ગાદી *f.*	*gādee*
custom-house	માંડવી *f.*	*mānḍvee*
departure	રવાનગી *f.*	*ruvāngee*
engine	અંજિન (*E*) *n.*	*unjin*
fare	ભાડું *n.*	*bẖāḍo͝on*
guard	ગાર્ડ (*E*) *m.*	*gārḍ*
guide	ભોમિયો *m.*	*bẖomiyo*
guide-book	માર્ગ-દર્શિકા *f.*	*mārg-durshikā*
hotel	વીશી *f.*	*veeshee*
interpreter	દુભાષિયો *m.*	*do͝obẖāshiyo*
key	કુંચી *f.*	*ko͝onchee*
landlady	વીશીવાળી *f.*	*veeshee-vāḷee*
landlord	વીશીવાળો *m.*	*veeshee-vāḷo*
luggage	સામાન *m.*	*sāmān*
office	ઓફિસ (*E*) *f.*	*ofis*
payment	ચુકાવો *m.*	*cho͝okāvo*
pilot	સુકાની *m.*	*so͝okānee*
porter	દરવાન, મજુર *m*	*durvān, mujo͝or*
railway	રેલવે (*E*) *f*	*relve*
railway carriage	આગગાડી *f.*	*āg-gāḍee*
,, station	સ્ટેશન (*E*) *n.*	*steshun*
receipt	રસીદ *f.*	*ruseed*
road	રસ્તો *m.*	*rusto*

English	Gujarati	Gujarati (romanized)
saddle	જીન *n.*	*jeen*
station-master	સ્ટેશન માસ્તર (*E*) *n.*	*steshun-māstur*
steamer	આગબોટ *f.*	*āg-bot*
strap	પટો *m.*	*puto*
ticket	ટિકેટ (*E*) *f.*	*tiket*
tent	તંબુ *m.*	*tunboo*
—pegs	મેખ *f.*	*mekh*
train	ટ્રેન (*E*), રેલગાડી *f.*	*tren, relgāḍee*
voyage	સફર *f.*	*sufur*
waiter	ખિદમતગાર *m.*	*khidmutgār*
whip	ચાબુક *m.*	*chābook*

Professions and Trades.

English	Gujarati	Gujarati (romanized)
Ambassador	એલચી *m.*	*elchee*
admiral	દરિયાઇ સેનાપતિ *m.*	*duriyāi senāputi*
agent	આડતિયો *m.*	*āḍutiyo*
aide-de-camp	નકીબ *m.*	*nukeeb*
artisan	કારિગર *m*	*kārigur*
astrologer	જોશી *m.*	*joshee*
astronomer	ખગોળવેત્તા *m.*	*khugoḷvettā*
atheist	નાસ્તિક *m.*	*māstik*
author	ગ્રંથકર્તા *m.*	*grunth-kurtā*
backbiter	ચાડિયો *m.*	*chāḍiyo*
baker	ભઠિયારો *m.*	*bhuthiyāro*
banker	નાણાવટી *m.*	*nāṇāvutee*
barber	હજામ *m.*	*hujām*
bard	ભાટ *m.*	*bhāt*
bird-catcher	વાઘરી *m.*	*vāghree*
blacksmith	લુહાર *m.*	*loohār*
brasier	કંસારો *m.*	*kunsāro*
broker	દલાલ *m.*	*dulāl*
butcher	કસાઇ *m.*	*kusāi*

English	Gujarati	Gujarati (romanized)
candidate	ઉમેદવાર *m.*	*oŏmedvār*
captain	કપ્તાન (*E*) *m.*	*kup'ān*
carder	પિંજારો *m.*	*pinjāro*
carpenter	સુતાર *m.*	*soŏtār*
chemist	રસાયણી *m.*	*rusāyunee*
clergyman	પાદરી *m.*	*pādree*
clerk	કારકુન *m.*	*kārkoŏn*
commander-in-chief	સેનાપતિ *m.*	*senāputi*
cobbler	ચમાર *m.*	*chumār*
confectioner	કંદોઇ *m.*	*kundoi*
contractor	ઇજારદાર *m*	*ijārdār*
cook	રસોયો *m.*	*rusoyo*
cowherd	ગોવાળ *m.*	*govāḷ*
cultivator	ખેડુત *m.*	*k̲h̲eḍoŏt*
customer	ઘરાક *n.*	*g̲h̲urāk*
doctor, physician	વૈદ્ય *m.*	*vaidy*
draper	કાપડિયો *m.*	*kāpuḍiyo*
druggist, grocer	ગાંધી *m.*	*gāndhee*
drummer	ઢોલી *m.*	*ḍ̲h̲olee*
dyer	રંગરેજ *m.*	*rungrej*
editor	અધિપતિ *m.*	*udhiputi*
farrier	નાલબંદ *m.*	*nālbund*
gardener	માળી *m.*	*mālee*
goldsmith	સોની *m.*	*sonee*
groom	ઘોડાવાળો *m.*	*g̲h̲oḍāvāḷo*
insolvent	દેવાળિયો *m.*	*devāḷiyo*
interpreter	દુભાષિયો *m.*	*doŏb̲h̲ās̲h̲iyo*
jeweller	ઝવેરી *m.*	*j̲h̲uveree*
judge	ન્યાયાધિશ *m*	*nyāyādhish*
juggler	મદારી *m.*	*mudāree*
labourer	મજૂર *m.*	*mujoor*

English	Gujarati	Gujarati (romanized)
land-holder	જાગીરદાર *m.*	*jāgeerdār*
laundress	ધોબણ *f.*	*dhobun*
lawyer	વકીલ *m.*	*vukeel*
liquor-vendor	કલાલ *m.*	*kulāl*
magician	જાદુગર *m.*	*jādoŏgur*
mathematician	ગણિત-વેત્તા *m.*	*gunit-vettā*
merchant	વેપારી *m.*	*vepāree*
messenger	ખેપિયો *m.*	*khepiyo*
midwife	સુયાણી .	*soŏyānee*
milkman	દૂધવાળો *m.*	*doodhvālo*
musician	ગવૈયો *m.*	*guvaiyo*
nurse	આયા *f.*	*āyā*
oilman	ઘાંચી *m.*	*ghānchee*
painter	ચિતારો *m.*	*chitāro*
pedlar	ફેરિયો *m.*	*feriyo*
partner	ભાગિયો *m.*	*bhāgiyo*
photographer	છબી પાડનાર *m.*	*chubee pādnar*
pirate	ચાંચિયો *m.*	*chānchiyo*
poet	કવિ *m.*	*kuvi*
potter	કુંભાર *m.*	*koŏnbhār*
prime minister	દીવાન, મુખ્ય-કારભારી *m.*	*deevān, moŏkhy kārbhāree*
printer	છાપનાર *m.*	*chāpnār*
reporter	ખબરપત્રી *m.*	*khuburputree*
robber	લૂટારો *m.*	*lootāro*
sailor	ખલાસી *m.*	*khulāsee*
scavanger	ભંગી *m.*	*bhungee*
servant	નોકર *m.*	*nokur*
shepherd	ભરવાડ *m.*	*bhurvād*
shoemaker	મોચી *m.*	*mochee*
stationer	કાગદી *m.*	*kāgdee*
tailor	દરજી *m.*	*durjee*

English	Gujarati	Gujarati (romanized)
teacher	શિક્ષક *m.*	*shiḵshuk*
tenant	ભાડૂત *m.*	*bhādoot*
tinman	કલઇગર *m.*	*kuluigur*
treasurer	ખજાનચી *m.*	*khujānchee*
washerman	ધોબી *m.*	*dholee*
watchmaker	ઘડિયાળી *m.*	*ghudiyāḷee*
watchman	પગી *m.*	*pugee*
weaver	વણકર *m.*	*vuṇkur*
woodcutter	કઠિયારો *m.*	*kuthiyāro*

Commercial Terms.

English	Gujarati	Gujarati (romanized)
Account	હિસાબ *m.*	*hisāb*
—current	ચાલુ હિસાબ *m*	*chāloŏ hisāb*
—, to close	હિસાબ બંધ કરવો *m.*	*hisāb bundh kurvo*
—, to settle	હિસાબ ચુકતો કરવો *m.*	*hisāb chŏokto kurvo*
—, of sale	વેચાણનો હિસાબ *m.*	*vechāṇ-no hisāb*
acknowledgement	પહોંચ *f.*	*puhonch*
advance (of money)	અગાઉથી આપેલા પૈસા *m. f.*	*ugā-ŏo-thee āpelā pāisā*
advice (letter of)	ખબર પત્ર *m.*	*khubur-putr*
agency	આડત *f.*	*āḍut*
agent	આડતિયો *m.*	*āḍutio*
apprentice	ઉમેદવાર *m.*	*ŏomedvār*
arrangement	ગોઠવણ *f.*	*gothvuṇ*
arrears	બાકી લહેણું *n.*	*bākee luheṇŏon*
assets	મિલ્કત *f.*	*milkut*
authorize, to	સત્તા આપવી *f.*	*suttā āpvee*
auction	હરરાજી, લીલામ *f. n.*	*hur-rājee, lilām*
average	સરેરાશ *f.*	*surerāsh*
balance	બાકી, સીલક *f.*	*bākee, shiluk*
balance-sheet	સરવૈયું *n.*	*survaiyŏon*
bank	શરાફી પેઢી *f.*	*shurāfee pedhee*
bale	ગાંસડી *f.*	*gānsudee*

English	Gujarati	Gujarati (romanized)
bargain	સાટું, સોદો *n., m.*	*sāṭoŏn, sodo*
bill	હુંડી *f.*	*hoŏnḍee*
book-keeper	નામાવાળો *m.*	*nāmāvāḷo*
brokerage	દલાલી *f.*	*dulālee*
business	ધંધો *m.*	*dhundho*
buyer	લેનાર *m.*	*lenār*
cargo	માલ, ભરતી *m., f.*	*māl, bhurtee*
catalogue	નોંધ, પત્રક *m. n.*	*nonth, putruk*
charter a ship, to	વહાણ ભાડે રાખવું *n.*	*vuhāṇ bhāḍe rākhuvoŏn*
claim	દાવો *m.*	*dāvo*
company	કંપની (*E*) *f.*	*kunpunee*
contract	કરાર, ઇજારો *m.*	*kurār, ijāro*
credit, on	ઉધારે *n.*	*oŏdhāre*
credit-balance	જમા રકમ *f.*	*jumā rukum*
customs duties	જકાત *f.*	*jukāt*
damages	નુકસાની *f.*	*noŏksānee*
,, to claim	નુકસાની માગવી *f.*	*noŏksānee māgvee*
date	મુદત *f.*	*moŏdut*
date, at 3 months'	ત્રણ મહિનાની મુદતની *f.*	*truṇ muhinānee moŏdutnee*
debit and credit	જમા ઉધાર *n.*	*jumā-oŏdhār*
demurrage	ડેમરેજ (*E*) *n.*	*ḍemrej*
discount	વળતર *n.*	*vuḷtur*
—, to	હુંડી વટાવવી *f.*	*hoŏnḍee vuṭāv-vee*
dividend	વહેંચણી *f.*	*vuhen hunṇe*
dock, harbour	ગોદી *f.*	*godee*
—dues	ગોદી ભાડું *n.*	*godee-bhāḍoŏn*
drawer (of bill)	હુંડી લખનાર *m.*	*hoŏnḍee lukhnār*
duty, export	જાવક દાણ *n.*	*jāvuk-dāṇ*
,, free	બિન જકાતી	*bin-jukātee*
—, import	આવક દાણ *n.*	*āvuk-dāṇ*

English	Gujarati	Gujarati (romanized)
duty, liable to	દાણપાત્ર	*dāṇ-pātr*
endorsement	શેરો *m.*	*shero*
exchange (of money)	લેવડ-દેવડ *f.*	*levuḍ-devuḍ*
factory	કારખાનું *n.*	*kār<u>kh</u>ānŏŏṅ*
firm	પેઢી *f.*	*pe<u>dh</u>ee*
forwarding agent	મારફતિયો *m.*	*mārfutiyo*
freight	નોર *n.*	*nor*
gross weight	સબાર્દાન તોલ *m*	*subārdān tol*
guarantee	જામીનગિરી *f.*	*jāmeengiree*
I. O. U.	મારે તમને દેવા છે	*māre tumne devā <u>ch</u>e*
import & export	આવક-જાવક *n.*	*āvuk-jāvuk*
income	પેદાશ *f.*	*pedāsh*
information	ખબર *m. p.*	*<u>kh</u>ubur*
insurance	વીમો *m.*	*veemo*
—policy	વીમા-ખત *n.*	*veemā-<u>kh</u>ut*
—premium	વીમાનો હફતો *m.*	*veemāno hufto*
insure against, to	વીમો ઉતરાવવો *m.*	*veemo ŏŏtrāv-vo*
interest	વ્યાજ *n.*	*vyāj*
liabilities	જવાબદારી *f.*	*juvābdāree*
manager	મેનેજર (*E*) *m.*	*menejur*
market	બજાર *f.*	*bujār*
—price	બજાર ભાવ *m.*	*bujār-<u>bh</u>āv*
package	દાગીનો *m.*	*dāgeeno*
payable to	જોગ	*jog*
per cent	ટકા *m. p.*	*tukā*
price	ભાવ *m.*	*b<u>h</u>āv*
—list	ભાવ-પત્રક *n.*	*<u>bh</u>āv-putruk*
—, net	ચોકખો ભાવ *m.*	*chok-<u>kh</u>o <u>bh</u>āv*
—, whole sale	સામટો ભાવ *m.*	*sāmto <u>bh</u>āv*
principal	મુદલ રકમ *f*	*mŏŏdul rukum*

English	Gujarati	Gujarati (romanized)
property	મિલ્કત *f.*	*milkut*
rate	ભાવ *m.*	*bhāv*
ready money	રોકડ *f.*	*rokud*
rent	ભાડું *n.*	*bhādoon*
retail	છૂટક *n.*	*chootuk*
—, to sell by	છૂટક વેચવું *n.*	*chootuk vechvoon*
settling day	પતવણીની મુદત	*putuvnee-nee moodut*
share	હિસ્સો, શેર (*E*) *m.*	*hisso, sher*
ship, to	વહાણ ભરવું *n.*	*vuhān bhurvoon*
solvent	સદ્ધર *m.*	*sudh-dhur*
stock	જથ્થો *m.*	*juth-tho*
—exchange	શેર બજાર *n.*	*sher-bujār*
trade	વેપાર *m.*	*vepār*
trustee	જુમેદાર, ટ્રસ્ટી (*E*) *m.*	*joomedār trustee*
under-writer	વીમો ઉતારનાર *m.*	*veemo-ootārnār*
usage	શિરસ્તો *m.*	*shirusto*
warehouse	વખાર *f.*	*vukhār*
wharf	ડક્કો *m.*	*dukko*
wharfage	ડક્કા-ભાડું *n*	*dukkā-bhādoon*
wholesale	સામટું *n.*	*sāmtoon*

Legal and Trading Terms.

English	Gujarati	Gujarati (romanized)
Accused	તોહમતદાર *m.*	*tohmutdār*
adopted son	દત્તપુત્ર *m.*	*duttpootr*
agreement	કરાર *m.*	*kurār*
argument	દલીલ *f.*	*duleel*
arbitrator	લવાદ, પંચ *m.*	*luvād, punch*
attachment	ટાંચ, જપ્તિ *f.*	*tānch, jupti*
attestation	શાખ *f.*	*shākh*
bail	જામીન *m.*	*jāmeen*
balance	શિલક *f*	*shiluk*
balance sheet	સરવૈયું *n*	*survaiyoon*

English	Gujarati	Gujarati (romanized)
bond	ખત *n.*	*k̲h̲ut*
capital	મૂડી *f.*	*mooḍee*
cash	રોકડ *f.*	*rokuḍ*
charter	પટ્ટો *m.*	*puṭṭo*
cheque	હુંડી *f.*	*hoŏnḍee*
civil	દિવાની *f.*	*divānee*
client	અસીલ *m.*	*useel*
commission	આડત *f*	*āḍut*
complaint	ફરિયાદ *f.*	*furiyād*
compromise	સમાધાની *f.*	*sumādhānee*
credit side	જમે બાજુ *f.*	*jume bājoŏ*
creditor	લહેણદાર *m.*	*luheṇdār*
criminal	ફોજદારી *f.*	*fojdāree*
day book	રોજ મેળ *m,*	*rojmeḷ*
debit side	ઉધાર બાજુ *f.*	*oŏdhar bāj[illegible]*
debt	કરજ *n.*	*kuruj*
debtor	કરજદાર *m.*	*kurujdār*
decree	હુકમનામું *n.*	*hoŏkumnāmoŏn*
deed of sale	કબાલો *m.*	*kubālo*
defamation	બદનકશી *f.*	*budnukshee*
defendant	પ્રતિવાદી *m.*	*prutivādee*
deposition	જુબાની *f.*	*joŏbānee*
discount	વટાવ *m.*	*vuṭāv*
divorce	તલાક, છૂટાછેડા *m. p.*	*tulāk, c̱hooṭāc̱heḍā*
document	દસ્તાવેજ *m.*	*dusṭāvej*
earnest money	બહાનું *n.*	*buhānoŏn*
estate	જાગીર *f.*	*jāgeer*
evidence	પુરાવો *m.*	*poŏrāvo*
excise, duty	જકાત, દાણ *f. n.*	*jukāt, dāṇ*
export	નિકાસ *f.*	*nikās*
gift	બક્ષિશ *f.*	*buk̲s̲h̲ish*
immovable property	સ્થાવર મિલ્કત *f.*	*sthāvur-milkut*

English	Gujarati	Gujarati (romanized)
import	આયાત *f.*	*āyāt*
income	આવક *f.*	*āvuk*
instalment	કાંધું, હફતો *n., m.*	*kandhoon. hufto*
insurance	વીમો *m.*	*veemo*
interest	વ્યાજ *n.*	*vyāj*
invoice	ભરતીયું *n.*	*bhurtiyoon*
judgment	ફેંસલો, ઠરાવ *m.*	*fenslo thurāv*
jury	પંચ *m. p.*	*punch*
justice	ઇન્સાફ, ન્યાય *m.*	*insāf, nyāy*
ledger	ખાતા વહી *f.*	*khkātāvuhee*
legacy	વારસો *m.*	*vārso*
license	પરવાનો *m.*	*purvāno*
liquidation	ફડચો *m.*	*fudcho*
loss	નુકસાન, ખોટ *n. f.*	*nooksān, khot*
maintenance	ભરણ-પોષણ *n.*	*bhurun-poshun*
memorandum	યાદી *f.*	*yādee*
monopoly	ઇજારો *m.*	*ijāro*
mortgage	ગીરો *n.*	*geero*
movable property	જંગમ મિલ્કત *f.*	*jungum-milkut*
murderer	ખુની *m.*	*khoonee*
oath	સોગંદ, પ્રતિજ્ઞા *m.p.f.*	*sogund, prutignā*
partnership	પંત્યાળું *n.*	*puntyāloon*
petition	અરજી *f.*	*urjee*
petitioner	અરજદાર *m.*	*urujdār*
plaintiff	વાદી *m.*	*vādee*
possession	કબજો *m.*	*kubjo*
postscript	તાજા કલમ *m. p.*	*tājākulum*
prisoner	કેદી *m.*	*kedee*
proclamation	ઢંઢેરો *m.*	*dhundhero*
profit	નફો *m.*	*nufo*
receipt	પહોંચ *f.*	[illegible]
release	ફારકતી *f.*	[illegible]

English	Gujarati	Gujarati (romanized)
sample	નમુનો *m.*	*numoŏno*
security	જામીનગિરી *f.*	*jāmeengiree*
signature	સહી *f.*	*suhee*
smuggling	દાણચોરી *f.*	*dāṇchoree*
suit	દાવો *m.*	*dāvo*
tax	કર, વેરો *m.*	*kur, vero*
transportation	દેશ નિકાલ *m.*	*desh nikāl*
witness	શાક્ષી *m.*	*shākshee*

Shooting and Fishing.

English	Gujarati	Gujarati (romanized)
Axe, hatchet	કુહાડી *f.*	*koŏhāḍee*
bait	ગલ *m.*	*gul*
barrel	નળી *f.*	*nuḷee*
boat	હોડી, મછવો *f., m.*	*hoḍee, muchvo*
boat-hook	હોડીનો આંકડો *m.*	*hoḍee-no-āṅkḍo*
boat-pole	હોડીનો વાંસડો	*hoḍee-no-vāṅsḍo*
boatman	ખારવો *m.*	*khārvo*
breech (of a gun)	કુંદો *m.*	*koŏṅlo*
bullet	ગોળી *f.*	*goḷee*
cartridge	કાર્તુસ *n.*	*kārtoŏs*
cord	રસી *f*	*rusee*
dagger	ખંજર *n.*	*khuṅjur*
double-barrelled	બે નળીની *f.*	*be nuḷeenee*
fish	માછલી *f.*	*māchulee*
—hook	કાંટો *m.*	*kāṅṭo*
fisherman	માછી માર *m.*	*mācheemār*
gimlet	સારડી *f.*	*sārḍee*
grindstone	સરાણ *f.*	*surāṇ*
gun	બંદૂક *f.*	*buṅdook*
gunpowder	દારૂ *m.*	*dāroŏ*
hammer	હથોડો *m.*	*huthoḍo*
hand-saw	હાથ-કરવત *m.*	*hāth-kurvut*
knife	છરી *f.*	*churee*

English	Gujarati	Gujarati (romanized)
matches	દિવાસળી *f. p*	*divāsulee*
nails	ખીલા *m. p.*	*kheelā*
net	જાળ *f.*	*jāl*
padlock	તાળું *n.*	*tālŏṅ*
pincers	ચિપિયો *m*	*chipiyo*
pistol	પિસ્તોલ (*E*) *f.*	*pistol*
ramrod	ગજ *m.*	*guj*
revolver	રિવોલ્વર (*E*) *f*	*rivolvur*
screw	પેચ *m.*	*pech*
screwdriver	ચાવી *f.*	*chāvee*
sheath	મિયાન *n.*	*miyān*
shooting	શિકાર-બાજી *f.*	*shikār-bājee*
shots	છરા *m. p.*	*churā*
sport	શિકાર *m.*	*shikār*
sportsman	શિકારી *m.*	*shikāree*
sword	તરવાર *f.*	*turvār*
tools	હથિયાર *n. p.*	*huthiyār*

Religious Terms.

English	Gujarati	Gujarati (romanized)
Alms	દાન *n.*	*dān*
angel	દેવદૂત *m.*	*dev-doot*
belief	શ્રદ્ધા *f.*	*shrud-dhā*
death	મોત, મરણ *n.*	*mot, muruṇ*
demon, devil	રાક્ષસ *m.*	*rākshus*
divine worship	પૂજા *f,*	*poojā*
doubt	શંકા *f.*	*shunkā*
everlasting	શાશ્વત	*shāshvut*
envy	ઇર્ષા *f.*	*irshā*
faith	આસ્થા *f.*	*āsthā*
fast	ઉપવાસ *m.*	*ŏŏpvās*
fear	ભય, ડર *m.*	*bhuy, dur*
forgiveness	ક્ષમા *f.*	*kshumā*
gladness	આનંદ *m.*	*ānund*

English	Gujarati	Gujarati (romanized)
hatred	દ્વેષ *m.*	*dvesh*
heart	હૃદય *n.*	*hruduy*
heaven	સ્વર્ગ *n.*	*svurg*
hell	નર્ક *n.*	*nurk*
holiness	પવિત્રતા *f.*	*puvitr-tā*
holy spirit	આત્મા *m.*	*ātmā*
honour	આબરૂ *f.*	*ābroŏ*
hope	આશા *f.*	*āshā*
ignominy	કલંક *n.*	*kulunk*
Jesus Christ	ઇસુ ખ્રિસ્ત *m.*	*isoŏ khrist*
knowledge	જ્ઞાન *n.*	*gnān*
life	જિંદગી *f.*	*jindgee*
love	પ્રેમ, રાગ *m.*	*prem, rāg*
may God preserve you	ઇશ્વર તમારૂં રક્ષણ-કરે	*ishvur tumāroŏn rukshuṇ kure*
mercy	દયા *f*	*duyā*
mind	મન, બુદ્ધિ *n., f.*	*mun, boŏd-dhi*
missionary	પાદરી *m.*	*pādree*
New Testament	નવો કરાર *m.*	*nuvo kurār*
Old Testament	જુનો કરાર *m.*	*joŏno kurār*
pain	દુખ *n.*	*doŏkh*
place of worship	મંદિર *n.*	*mundir*
please God	ઇશ્વરેચ્છા *f.*	*ishvur- -ch-chā*
peace	શાંતિ *f.*	*shānti*
praise	સ્તુતિ *f.*	*stoŏti*
prayer	પ્રાર્થના *f.*	*prārthnā*
psalm	ભજન *n.*	*bhujun*
religion	ધર્મ *m*	*dhurm*
right, justice	ન્યાય *m.*	*nyāy*
righteousness	સદાચાર *m.*	*sudāchār*
saint	સાધુ *m.*	*sādhoŏ*
salvation	મુક્તિ *f.*	*moŏkti*

English	Gujarati	Gujarati (romanized)
sin	પાપ *n.*	*pāp*
sorrow	ખેદ, કલેશ *m.*	*khed, klesh*
soul, spirit	જીવ, આત્મા *m.*	*jeev, ātmā*
temptation	લાલચ *f.*	*lāluch*
thought	વિચાર *m.*	*vichār*
trust	વિશ્વાસ, શ્રદ્ધા *m., f.*	*vishvās, shruddhā*
wisdom	ડહાપણ *n.*	*duhāpuṇ*
word of God	ઇશ્વર-વચન *n.*	*ishvur-vuchun*
worship of God	ઇશ્વ-ભક્તિ *f.*	*ishvur-bhukti*
worshipper of God	ઇશ્વર-ભક્ત *m.*	*ishvur-bhukt*
wrong-doing	અધર્મ *m.*	*udhurm*
The Hindu Trinity	ત્રિમૂર્તિ *f.*	*trimoorti*
The Creator	બ્રહ્મા *m.*	*bruhmā*
The Preserver	વિષ્ણુ *m.*	*vishṇoŏ*
The Destroyer	મહેશ *m.*	*muhesh*

Miscellaneous Words.

English	Gujarati	Gujarati (romanized)
Address	સરનામું, માનપત્ર *n.*	*surnāmoŏn, mān-putr*
anchor	લંગર *n.*	*lungur*
bridge	પુલ *m.*	*poŏl*
building	મકાન *n.*	*mukān*
bush	ઝાડી *f.*	*jhāḍee*
cattle	ઢોર *n. p.*	*dhor*
chariot	રથ *m.*	*ruth*
church	દેવળ *n.*	*devuḷ*
coffee-house	ઘાવાખાનું *n.*	*ghāvā-khānoŏn*
courtyard	ચોક *m.*	*chok*
date	તારીખ *f.*	*tāreekh*
deck	તુતક *n.*	*toŏtuk*
ditch	ખાઇ *f.*	*khāi*

English	Gujarati	Gujarati (romanized)
edifice	ઇમારત *f.*	*imārut*
envelope	કવર *n*	*kuvur*
fence	વાડ *f.*	*vāḍ*
field, farm	ખેતર *n.*	*k̲h̲etur*
fine	દંડ *m.*	*dunḍ*
flag	વાવટો *m.*	*vāvṭo*
—staff	વાવટા-કાઠી *f.*	*vāvṭā-kāṭ̲h̲ee*
footpath	કેડી *f.*	*keḍee*
forest, wood	જંગલ *n.*	*jungul*
grass	ઘાસ *n.*	*g̲h̲ās*
guest	મહેમાન	*muhemān*
happiness	સુખ *n.*	*sŏŏk̲h̲*
hay	ખડ *n.*	*k̲h̲uḍ*
highroad	રાજમાર્ગ *m.*	*rājmārg*
hospital	દવાખાનું *n.*	*duvā-k̲h̲ānŏŏn*
hut	ઝુંપડું *n.*	*j̲h̲ŏŏnpuḍŏŏn*
ink	શાહી *f.*	*shāhee*
inn	ધર્મશાળા *f.*	*dhurm-shāḷā*
joy	આનંદ *m.*	*ānund*
lane, street	શેરી *f.*	*sheree*
letter-box	ટપાલની પેટી *f.*	*ṭupāl-nee-peṭee*
misery	દુખ *n.*	*dŏŏk̲h̲*
mosque	મસ્જિદ *f.*	*musjid*
murder	ખુન *n.*	*k̲h̲ŏŏn*
nib	ટાંક *f.*	*ṭānk*
palace	મહેલ *m.*	*muhel*
peace	શાંતિ, સલાહ *f.*	*shānti, sulāh̲*
post	ટપાલ *f.*	*ṭupāl*
—man	ટપાલવાળો *m.*	*ṭupāl-vāḷo*
—master	ટપાલ માસ્તર	*ṭupāl-māsṭur*
—office	ટપાલ ઑફિસ *f.*	*ṭupāl ofis*
prison	કેદખાનું *n.*	*ked-k̲h̲ānŏŏn*

English	Gujarati	Gujarati (romanized)
public-ho	પીઠું *n.*	*peet̲h̲ŏŏn*
right	હક *m.*	*huk*
rope	દોરડું *n.*	*dorḍŏŏn*
school	નિશાળ *f.*	*nishāḷ*
—master	મહેતાજી *m.*	*muhetājee*
seal	મહોર *f*	*muhor*
sealing wax	લાખ *f.*	*lāk̲h̲*
ship	વહાણ *n.*	*vuh iṇ*
shop	દુકાન *f.*	*dŏŏkān*
telegram	તાર *m.*	*tār*
temple	મંદિર *n.*	*mundir*
theatre	નાટકશાળા *f.*	*nāṭukshāḷā*
timber	કાટ *m.*	*kāṭ*
tomb	કબર *f.*	*kubur*
tower	બુરજ *m.*	*bŏŏruj*
townhall	પુર-ગૃહ *n.*	*pŏŏr-gruh*
tree	ઝાડ *n.*	*j̲h̲āḍ*
university	પાઠશાળા *f.*	*pāt̲h̲-shāḷá*
writing	અક્ષર *m. p.*	*uk̲s̲h̲ur*

Cardinal Numbers.

English figures	Gujarati figures	Gujarati	Gujarati (romanized)
1	૧	એક	*ek*
2	૨	બે	*be*
3	૩	ત્રણ	*truṇ*
4	૪	ચાર	*chār*
5	૫	પાચ	*pànch*
6	૬	છ	*c̲h̲*
7	૭	સાત	*sāt*
8	૮	આઠ	*āt̲h̲*
9	૯	નવ	*nuv*
10	૧૦	દસ	*dus*

English figures	Gujarati figures	Gujarati	Gujarati (romanized)
11	૧૧	અગિયાર	*ugiyār*
12	૧૨	બાર	*bār*
13	૧૩	તેર	*ter*
14	૧૪	ચૌદ	*chowd*
15	૧૫	પંદર	*puṁdur*
16	૧૬	સોળ	*soḷ*
17	૧૭	સત્તર	*suttur*
18	૧૮	અઢાર	*udhār*
19	૧૯	ઓગણીસ	*oguṇees*
20	૨૦	વીસ	*vees*
21	૨૧	એકવીસ	*ekvees*
22	૨૨	બાવીસ	*bāvees*
23	૨૩	ત્રેવીસ	*trevees*
24	૨૪	ચોવીસ	*chovees*
25	૨૫	પચીસ	*puchees*
26	૨૬	છવીસ	*chuvees*
27	૨૭	સત્તાવીસ	*suttāvees*
28	૨૮	અઠાવીસ	*uthāvees*
29	૨૯	ઓગણત્રીસ	*oguṇ-trees*
30	૩૦	ત્રીસ	*trees*
31	૩૧	એકત્રીસ	*ektrees*
32	૩૨	બત્રીસ	*butrees*
33	૩૩	તેત્રીસ	*tetrees*
34	૩૪	ચોત્રીસ	*chotrees*
35	૩૫	પાંત્રીસ	*pāntrees*
36	૩૬	છત્રીસ	*chutrees*
37	૩૭	સાડત્રીસ	*sāḍtrees*
38	૩૮	આડત્રીસ	*āḍtrees*
39	૩૯	ઓગણચાલીસ	*oguṇ-chālees*
40	૪૦	ચાલીસ	*chālees*
41	૪૧	એકતાલીસ	*ektālees*
42	૪૨	બેંતાલીસ	*beṅtālees*

English figures	Gujarati figures	Gujarati	Gujarati (romanized)
43	૪૩	ત્રેતાલીસ	*tretālees*
44	૪૪	ચુમાલીસ	*choŏmālees*
45	૪૫	પિસ્તાલીસ	*pistālees*
46	૪૬	છેંતાલીસ	*chentālees*
47	૪૭	સુડતાલીસ	*soŏḍtālees*
48	૪૮	અડતાલીસ	*uḍtālees*
49	૪૯	ઓગણપચાસ	*oguṇ-puchās*
50	૫૦	પચાસ	*puchās*
51	૫૧	એકાવન	*ekāvun*
52	૫૨	બાવન	*bāvun*
53	૫૩	ત્રેપન	*trepun*
54	૫૪	ચોપન	*chopun*
55	૫૫	પંચાવન	*punchāvun*
56	૫૬	છપન	*chupun*
57	૫૭	સત્તાવન	*suttāvun*
58	૫૮	અઠાવન	*uthāvun*
59	૫૯	ઓગણસાઠ	*oguṇ-sāth*
60	૬૦	સાઠ	*sāth*
61	૬૧	એકસઠ	*eksuth*
62	૬૨	બાસઠ	*bāsuth*
63	૬૩	ત્રેસઠ	*tresuth*
64	૬૪	ચોસઠ	*chosuth*
65	૬૫	પાંસઠ	*pānsuth*
66	૬૬	છાસઠ	*chāsuth*
67	૬૭	સડસઠ	*suḍsuth*
68	૬૮	અડસઠ	*uḍsuth*
69	૬૯	ઓગણોતેર	*ogṇoter*
70	૭૦	સિત્તેર	*sitter*
71	૭૧	એકોતેર	*ekoter*
72	૭૨	બોંતેર	*bonter*
73	૭૩	તોંતેર	*tonter*
74	૭૪	ચુમોતેર	*choŏmoter*

English figures	Gujarati figures	English	Gujarati (romanized)
75	૭૫	પંચોતેર	*puṅchoter*
76	૭૬	છોંતેર	*c̲h̲oṅter*
77	૭૭	સત્તોતેર	*suttoter*
78	૭૮	અઠોતેર	*ut̲h̲oter*
79	૭૯	ઓગણાએંશી	*ogṇā-eṅshee*
80	૮૦	એંશી	*eṅshee*
81	૮૧	એકાશી	*ekāshee*
82	૮૨	બાશી	*bāshee*
83	૮૩	તાશી	*tāshee*
84	૮૪	ચોરાશી	*chorāshee*
85	૮૫	પંચાશી	*upṅchāshee*
86	૮૬	છાશી	*c̲h̲āshee*
87	૮૭	સત્તાશી	*suttashee*
88	૮૮	અઠાશી	*ut̲h̲ashee*
89	૮૯	નેવાશી	*nevāshee*
90	૯૦	નેવું	*nevŏŏṅ*
91	૯૧	એકાણું	*ekāṇŏŏṅ*
92	૯૨	બાણું	*bāṇŏŏṅ*
93	૯૩	ત્રાણું	*trāṇŏŏṅ*
94	૯૪	ચોરાણું	*chorāṇŏŏṅ*
95	૯૫	પંચાણું	*puṅchaṇŏŏṅ*
96	૯૬	છનું	*c̲h̲unŏŏṅ*
97	૯૭	સત્તાણું	*suttāṇŏŏṅ*
98	૯૮	અઠાણું	*ut̲h̲āṇŏŏṅ*
99	૯૯	નવાણું	*nuvāṇŏŏṅ*
100	૧૦૦	સો	*so*
1000	૧૦૦૦	હજાર	*hujūr*
100000	૧૦૦૦૦૦	લાખ	*lāk̲h̲*
10000000	૧૦૦૦૦૦૦૦	કરોડ	*kuroḍ*
$\frac{1}{4}$	૦।	પા	*pā*
$\frac{1}{2}$	૦॥	અરધો	*urdho*
$\frac{3}{4}$	૦।॥	પોણો	*poṇo*

English figures	Gujarati figures	Gujarati	Gujarati (romanized).
$1\frac{1}{4}$	૧।	સવા	*suvā*
$1\frac{1}{2}$	૧॥	દોઢ	*dodh*
$1\frac{3}{4}$	૧।	પોણાબે	*poṇā-be*
$2\frac{1}{4}$	૨।	સવાબે	*suvā-be*
$2\frac{1}{2}$	૨॥	અઢી	*udhee*
$3\frac{1}{2}$	૩॥	સાડાત્રણ	*sāḍā-truṇ*

Ordinal Numbers.

English	Gujarati	Gujarati (romanized)
First	પહેલો *d.**	*puhelo*
second	બીજો *d.*	*beejo*
third	ત્રીજો *d*	*treejo*
fourth	ચોથો *d*	*chotho*
fifth	પાંચમો *d*	*pānchmo*
sixth	છઠો *d.*	*chhutho*
seventh	સાતમો *d.*	*satmo*

Note—From seventh upwards the ordinal numbers are expressed by adding મો, મી, મું, (*mo, mee, moon*) to the cardinal number, according to the gender of the noun to which they are prefixed or suffixed as સાતમી ચોપડી, (*sātmee chopḍee*) the seventh book.

The multiplicatives are expressed by adding ગણા (*guṇā*) to the cardinal number as સાત ગણા, *sāt-guṇā*, seventimes.

Pronouns.

English	Gujarati	Gujarati (romanized)
A few	થોડા *d.*	*thoḍā*
any	કોઇ *ind.*†	*koi*
anyone	હરકોઇ *ind.*	*hur-koi*
each	દરેક *ind.*	*durek*

* declinable

† indeclinable

English	Gujarati	Gujarati (romanized)
each-other	એકબીજા *d.*	*ek-beejā*
every	દરેક *ind.*	*durek*
how big	કેવડું *d*	*kevuḍŏon*
how many	કેટલા *d.*	*keṭlā*
how much	કેટલું *d.*	*keṭlŏon*
little	થોડું *d.*	*thoḍŏon*
self	પોતે *ind.*	*pote*
some (number)	થોડાક *d.*	*thoḍāk*
some (quantity)	થોડુંક *ind.*	*thoḍŏonk*
something	કાંઇક *ind.*	*kān-ik*
so many	આટલા *d.*	*āṭlā*
so much	આટલું *ind.*	*āṭlŏon*
that	પેલું *d.*	*pelŏon*
this	આ *ind.*	*ā*
what (inter)	શું *d.*	*shŏon*
,, (rel)	જે-તે *ind.*	*je-te*
which (inter)	કયું *d.*	*kuyŏon*
,, (rel)	જે-તે *ind.*	*je-te*
who (inter)	કોણ *ind.*	*koṇ*
,, (rel)	જે *ind.*	*je*
whom (inter)	કોને *ind.*	*kone*
,, (rel)	જેને *ind.*	*jene*
whose (inter)	કોનું *d.*	*konŏon*
,, (rel)	જેનું *d.*	*jenŏon*
whosoever	જે કોઇ *ind.*	*je-koi*

Adjectives.

Bad	ખરાબ *ind.*	*k͟hurāb*
beautiful	ખુબસૂરત *ind.*	*k͟hŏob-soorut*
bitter	કડવું *d.*	*kuḍvŏon*
black	કાળું *d*	*kāḷŏon*
blind	આંધળો *d.*	*āndhḷo*
blue	વાદળી *ind.*	*vādḷee*

English	Gujarati	Gujarati (romanized
bold, brave	બહાદુર *ind.*	*buhādoŏr*
brown	ભુરો *d.*	*bhoŏro*
broad	પહોળો *d.*	*puholo*
cheap	સસ્તું *d.*	*sustoŏn*
clever	હોશિયાર *ind.*	*hoshiyār*
cold	ઠંડો *d.*	*thundo*
deaf	બહેરો *d.*	*buhero*
dark	અંધારો, ઘેરો *d.*	*undhāro, ghero*
dear, costly	મોંઘું *d.*	*monghoŏn*
dirty	ગંદું *d.*	*gundoŏn*
dry	સૂકું *d.*	*sookoŏn*
dumb	મૂંગો *d.*	*moongo*
easy	સહેલો *d.*	*sukelo*
false	જુઠો *d.*	*joŏtho*
fat	જાડો *d.*	*jādo*
feeble, lean	દુબળો *d.*	*doŏblo*
fierce	વિકરાળ *ind.*	*vikral*
fit, worthy	લાયક *ind.*	*lāyuk*
foolish, stupid	મૂર્ખ *ind.*	*moorkh*
fresh	તાજું *d.*	*tājoŏn*
full	ભરપુર *ind.*	*bhurpoŏr*
gay	આનંદી *ind.*	*ānundee*
gentle, mild	નમ્ર *ind.*	*numr*
good	સારો, ભલો *d.*	*sāro, bhulo*
great, large	મોટો *d.*	*moto*
green	લીલો *d.*	*leelo*
happy	સુખી *ind.*	*soŏkhee*
hard	સખત *ind.*	*sukhut*
heavy	ભારે *ind.*	*bhāre*
high	ઉંચો *d.*	*oŏncho*
hollow	પોલો *d.*	*polo*
honest	પ્રમાણિક *ind.*	*prumāṇik*

English	Gujarati	Gujarati (romanized)
hungry	ભૂખ્યો *d.*	*bhookhyo*
ill, sick	માંદો *d.*	*māndo*
innocent	નિર્દોષ *ind.*	*nirdosh*
just	વાજબી *ind.*	*vājbee*
lame	લંગડો *d.*	*lungdo*
long	લાંબું *d.*	*lānboon*
narrow	સાંકડું *d.*	*sānkdoon*
naughty	તોફાની *ind.*	*tofānee*
new	નવું *d.*	*nuvoon*
old	જુનું, ઘરડું *d*	*joonoon, ghurdoon*
polite	વિવેકી *ind.*	*vivekee*
poor	ગરીબ *ind.*	*gureeb*
pretty, fair	સુંદર *ind.*	*soondur*
private	ખાનગી *ind.*	*khāngee*
proud	મગરૂર *ind.*	*mugroor*
pure, clean	સાફ *ind.*	*sāf*
quiet	શાંત *ind.*	*shānt*
red	લાલ *ind.*	*lāl*
rich	પૈસાદાર *ind.*	*paisādār*
ripe	પાકું *d.*	*pākoon*
round	ગોળ *ind.*	*gol*
sharp, swift	તેજ *ind.*	*tej*
short	ટુંકું *d.*	*toonkoon*
slow	ધીમો *d.*	*dheemo*
small	નાનું *d.*	*nānoon*
smooth	લીસું *d.*	*leesoon*
soft	નરમ *ind.*	*nurum*
sour	ખાટું *n.*	*khātoon*
strong	મજબૂત *in*	*mujboot*
sweet	મીઠું *d.*	*meethoon*
thick	જાડું *d.*	*jādoon*
thin	પાતળું *d.*	*pātloon*

English	Gujarati	Gujarati (romanized)
thirsty	તરસ્યો *d.*	*tursyo*
true	સાચો, ખરો *d.*	*sācho, k̲h̲uro*
useful	ઉપયોગી *ind.*	*o͝opyogee*
warm, hot	ગરમ *ind.*	*gurum*
weak	નબળો *p.*	*nubḷo*
wet	ભીનો *d.*	*b̲h̲eeno*
white	ધોળો *d.*	*dhoḷo*
whole	આખો *d.*	*āk̲h̲o*
wide	પહોળો *d.*	*puhoḷo*
wise	ડાહ્યો *d.*	*ḍāhyo*
yellow	પીળો *d.*	*peeḷo*

Verbs.

Note:--Most of the Gujarati verbs are formed by prefixing a noun or an adjective to a verb, as જવાબ આપવો, *juvāb āpvo*, to (give) answer; માંદા પડવું, *mā̃ndā puḍvo͝on*, to fall ill.

The following are the chief auxiliaries used:—

કરવું, *kurvo͝on*, to do; આપવું, *āpvo͝on*, to give
લેવું, *levo͝on*, to take; દેવું, *devo͝on*, to give
થવું, હોવું, *thuvo͝on*, *hovo͝on*, to be; જવુ, *juvo͝on*, to go
રાખવું, *rāk̲h̲vo͝on*, to keep; કહેવું, *kuhevo͝on*, to say.

English	Gujarati	Gujarati (romanized)
Able, to be	શકવું	*shuk.o͝on*
acknowledge, admit	કબુલ કરવું	*kubo͝ol kurvo͝on*
accept	સ્વીકારવું	*sveekārvo͝on*
acquire, get	મેળવવું	*meḷuv-vo͝on*
admit	દાખલ કરવુ	*dāk̲h̲ul kurvo͝on*
admire, praise	વખાણવું	*vuk̲h̲āṇvo͝on*
advice	સલાહ આપવી	*sulāh āpvee*

English	Gujarati	Gujarati (romaniz
agree	મળતા થવું	*multā thuvoǒn*
allow, let	દેવું	*devoǒn*
answer, reply	જવાબ દેવો	*juvāb devo*
appear, look	દેખાવું	*dekhāi oǒn*
approve	પસંદ કરવું	*pusund kurvoǒn*
arrange	ગોઠવવું	*gothuv-voǒn*
arrive, reach	પહોંચવું	*puhonch-voǒn*
ascend	ચઢવું	*chudhvoǒn*
ask, inquire	પૂછવું	*pooch oǒn*
assure	ખાતરી આપવી	*khātree-āpvee*
awake	જાગવું	*jāgvoǒn*
be, become	થવું હોવું,	*thuvoǒn hovoǒn*
beat	મારવું	*mārvoǒn*
beg	માંગવું	*māgvoǒn*
begin	શરૂ કરવું	*shuroǒ kurvoǒn*
believe	માનવું	*mānvoǒn*
blame, rebuke	ઠપકો આપવો	*thupko āpvo*
besiege	ઘેરો ઘાલવો	*ghero ghālvo*
boil	ઉકાળવું	*oǒkālvoǒn*
borrow	ઉછીનું લેવું	*oǒchheenoǒn levoǒn*
bring	લાવવું	*lāv-voǒn*
build	બાંધવું	*bāndhvoǒn*
buy, purchase	ખરીદ કરવું	*khureed-kurvoǒn*
call	બોલાવવું	*bolāv-voǒn*
carry	લઇ જવું	*lui-juvoǒn*
catch, seize	પકડવું	*pukudvoǒn*
come	આવવું	*āvuvoǒn*
complain	ફરિયાદ કરવી	*furiyād kurvee*
confused, to be	ગભરાઇ જવું	*gubhrāi juvoǒn*
consent	કબુલ કરવું	*kuboǒl kurvoǒn*
continue	ચાલુ રાખવું	*chāloǒ rākhvoǒn*
cook	રાંધવું	*rāndhvoǒn*

English	Gujarati	Gujarati (romanized)
copy	નકલ કરવી	*nukul kurvee*
correct	સુધારવું	*soŏdhārvoŏn*
count	ગણવું	*gun̤voŏn*
cover	ઢાંકવું	*d̲h̲ānkvoŏn*
create	પેદા કરવું	*pedā kurvoŏn*
cured, to be	સાજા થવું	*sājā thuvoŏn*
dance	નાચવું	*nāchvoŏn*
deceive, cheat	છેતરવું	*c̲h̲eturvoŏn*
delay	ઢીલ કરવી	*d̲h̲eel kurvee*
delighted, to be	ખુશી થવું	*k̲h̲ooshee thuvoon*
deny	ના પાડવી	*nā pād̤vee*
depart	ચાલ્યા જવું	*chālyā juvoŏn*
descend	ઉતરવું	*ŏoturvoŏn*
describe	વર્ણન કરવુ	*vurn̤un kurvoŏn*
deserve	લાયક થવું	*lāyuk thuvoŏn*
desire, wish	ઇચ્છવું	*ich-c̲h̲voŏn*
destroy	નાશ કરવો	*nāsh kurvo*
die	મરી જવું	*muree juvoŏn*
dig	ખોદવું	*k̲h̲odvoŏn*
dine, sup	જમવું	*jumvoŏn*
disappear, to be lost	ગુમ થવું	*goŏm thuvoŏn*
discharge, acquit	છોડી મૂકવું	*c̲h̲od̤ee mookvoŏn*
do	કરવું	*kurvoŏn*
draw, pull	ખેંચવુ	*k̲h̲enchvoŏn*
dress	કપડાં પહેરવાં	*kupd̤ān puhervān*
drink	પીવું	*peevoŏn*
eat	ખાવું	*h̲h̲āvoŏn*
engaged, to be	કામમાં હોવું	*kām-mān hovoŏn*
enjoy	ભોગવવું	*b̲h̲oguv-voŏn*
examine, inspect	તપાસવું	*tupāsvoŏn*
exchange	બદલાવવું	*budlāv-voŏn*

English	Gujarati	Gujarati (romanized)
excuse, pardon	માફ કરવું	*māf kurvo͝on*
exclaim	બોલી ઉઠવું	*bolee o͝oṯẖvo͝on*
explain	સમજાવવું	*sumjāv-vo͝on*
expose	ખુલ્લું કરવું	*k̲h̲o͝ollo͝on kurvo͝on*
fall	પડવું	*puḍvo͝on*
feel	લાગવું	*lāgvo͝on*
fight	લડવું	*luḍvo͝on*
find	શોધવું	*shodhvo͝on*
finish	પૂરૂ કરવું	*pooro͝on kurvo͝on*
flow	વહેવું	*vuhevo͝on*
follow	પાછળ આવવું	*pāc̲h̲uḷ āvuvo͝on*
found	સ્થાપવું	*sthāpvo͝on*
forget	ભૂલી જવુ	*b̲h̲oolee juvo͝on*
get, obtain	મેળવવું	*meḷuv-vo͝on*
give	આપવું	*āpvo͝on*
go	જવું	*juvo͝on*
go away	ચાલ્યા જવું	*chālyā juvo͝on*
grow	ઉગવું, વધવું	*o͝ogvo͝on, vudhvo͝on*
hate, despise	ધિક્કારવું	*dhikkārvo͝on*
hear	સાંભળવું	*sānb̲h̲uḷvo͝on*
heed, attend to	ધ્યાન આપવું	*dhyān āpho͝on*
hide	સંતાડવું	*suntāḍvo͝on*
hire	ભાડે રાખવું	*b̲h̲āḍe rāk̲h̲vo͝on*
hold	પકડી રાખવું	*pukḍee rāk̲h̲vo͝on*
hope	આશા રાખવી	*āshā rāk̲h̲vee*
imagine, suppose	ધારવું	*dhārvo͝on*
insult	અપમાન કરવુ	*upmān kurvo͝on*
invite	આમંત્રણ કર	*āmuntruṇ kurvo͝on*
joke	મશ્કરી કરવી	*mushkuree kurvee*
jump	કૂદવું	*koodvo͝on*
keep	રાખવું	*rāk̲h̲vo͝on*
know	જાણવું	*jāṇvo͝on*

English	Gujarati	Gujarati (romanized)
laugh, smile	હસવું	*husvoŏn*
learn	શીખવું	*sheekhvoŏn*
lend	ઉછીનું આપવું	*oŏcheenoŏn āpvoŏn*
lie down	પડી રહેવું	*pudee ruhevoŏn*
lift	ઉચકવું	*oŏchukvoŏn*
light, kindle	સળગાવવું	*sulgāv-voŏn*
like	ચાહવું	*chāhvoŏn*
listen	સાંભળવું, માનવું	*sāṅbhulvoŏn mānvoŏn*
live	રહેવું	*ruhevoŏn*
look, see	જોવું	*jovoŏn*
lose	ખોવું	*khovoŏn*
love	ચાહવું	*chāhvoŏn*
maintain, support	ભરણ-પોષણ કરવું	*bhuruṇ-poshuṇ kurvoŏn*
make	બનાવવું	*bunāv-voŏn*
meet, see	મળવું	*mulvoŏn*
melt	ગાળવું	*gālvoŏn*
mend	સુધારવું	*soŏdharvoŏn*
move	ખસવું, ખસેડવું	*khusvoŏn, khused-voŏn*
oblige	મહેરબાની કરવી	*muherbānee kurvee*
offend	ગુસ્સે કરવું	*goŏsse kurvoŏn*
offended, to be	ગુસ્સે થવું	*goŏsse thuvoŏn*
open	ઉઘાડવું	*oŏghādvoŏn*
paint	રંગવું	*rungvoŏn*
pay	પૈસા આપવા	*paisā āpvā*
plant	વાવવું, રોપવું	*vāv-voŏn, ropvoŏn*
play	રમવું	*rumvoŏn*
pluck	ચુંટવું	*choŏntvoŏn*
pray	પ્રાર્થના કરવી	*prārthnā kurvee*
prevent	અટકાવવું	*utkāv-voŏn*

English	Gujarati	Gujarati (romanized)
prove	સાબિત કરવું	*sābit kurvoo̐n*
punish	સજા કરવી	*sujā kurvee*
put	મૂકવું	*mookvoo̐n*
quarrel	કજિયો કરવો	*kujiyo kurvo*
read	વાંચવું	*vānchvoo̐n*
reap	લણવું	*luṇvoo̐n*
refuse	ના પાડવી	*nā pāḍvee*
regret	દિલગીર થવું	*dilgeer thuvoo̐n*
rejoice	ખુશી થવું	*k͟hooshee thuvoo̐n*
remain	રહેવું	*ruhevoo̐n*
remember	યાદ રાખવું	*yād rāk͟hvoo̐n*
repay, return	પાછું આપવું	*pāc͟hoo̐n āpvoo̐n*
repeat	ફરીથી બોલવું	*fureethee bolvoo̐n*
repent	પસ્તાવું	*pustavoo̐n*
rest, repose	આરામ લેવો	*ārām levo*
return	પાછા આવવું	*pāc͟hā āv-voo̐n*
ring	વગાડવું	*vugāḍvoo̐n*
rub	ઘસવું	*g͟husvoo̐n*
run	દોડવું	*doḍvoo̐n*
run away	નાશી જવું	*nāshee juvoo̐n*
save	બચાવવું	*buchāv-voo̐n*
see	જોવું, મળવું	*jovoo̐n, muḷvoo̐n*
seek, search	શોધવું	*shodhvoo̐n*
sell	વેચવું	*vechvoo̐n*
send	મોકલવું	*mokulvoo̐n*
send for	મંગાવવું. તેડાવવું	*mungāv-voo̐n, teḍāv-voo̐n*
serve	નોકરી કરવી	*nokree kurvee*
serve (dinner)	પીરસવું	*peerusvoo̐n*
set out	રવાના થવું	*ruvānā thuvoo̐n*
shake	હલવું, હલાવવું	*hulvoo̐n, hulāv-voo̐n*

English	Gujarati	Gujarati (romanized)
shine	પ્રકાશવું	*prukāshvoŏn*
shoot	ગોળીએ મારવું	*golee-e mārvoŏn*
show	બતાવવું	*butāv-voŏn*
shut	બંધ કરવું	*bundh kurvoŏn*
sign	સહી કરવી	*suhee kurvee*
sit	બેસવું	*besvoŏn*
sleep	ઉંઘવું, સુવું	*oŏnghvoŏn, soŏvoŏn*
smile	હસવું	*husvoŏn*
sow	વાવવું	*vāv-voŏn*
speak	બોલવું	*bolvoŏn*
spin	કાતવું	*kāntvoŏn*
stand	ઉભા થવું	*oŏbhā thuvoŏn*
starve	ભૂખે મરવું	*bhookhe murvoŏn*
stay	રહેવું	*rukevoŏn*
steal	ચોરવું	*chorvoŏn*
stitch, sew	શીવવું	*sheev-voŏn*
stop	અટકવું, અટકાવવું	*utukvoŏn, utkāv-voŏn*
study, learn	ભણવું	*bhunrvoŏn*
succeed	ફાવવું	*fāv-voŏn*
support	પાળવું	*pālvoŏn*
swear	સોગંદ ખાવા	*sogund khāvā*
swim	તરવું	*turvoŏn*
take	લેવું	*levoŏn*
talk, chat	વાત કરવી	*vāt kurvee*
taste	ચાખવું	*chākh[illegible]*
tell, say	કહેવું	*kuh[illegible]*
thank	આભાર માનવો	*ābh[illegible] ān[illegible]*
think	વિચાર કરવો	*vich[illegible] [illegible]voo*
throw	ફેંકવું	*feinkvoŏn*
tie	બાંધવું	*bāndhvoŏn*
touch	અડકવું	*udukvoŏn*

English	Gujarati	Gujarati (romanized)
translate	તરજુમો કરવો	*turjoŏmo kurvo*
travel	મુસાફરી કરવી	*moŏsāfuree kurvee*
try, strive	યત્ન કરવો	*yutn kurvo*
understand	સમજવું	*sumujvoŏn*
use	વાપરવું	*vāpurvoŏn*
wait	રાહ જોવી	*rāh jovee*
walk	ચાલવું	*chālvoŏn*
want, require	જરૂર હોવી, માગવું	*juroŏr hovee, māgvoŏn*
warn	ચેતવણી આપવી	*chetuvuṇee āpvee*
wash	ધોવું	*dhovoŏn*
waste	ગુમાવવું	*goŏmāv-voŏn*
weep, cry	રડવું	*ruḍvoŏn*
weave	વણવું	*vuṇvoŏn*
weigh	તોળવું, વજન કરવું	*toḷvoŏn vujun kurvoŏn*
welcome	આવકાર આપવો	*āvkār āpvo*
wish	ઇચ્છવું	*ich-chvoŏn*
work	કામ કરવું	*kām kurvoŏn*
worship	પુજા કરવી	*poŏjā kurvee*
write	લખવું	*lukhvoŏn*

Adverbs, Conjunctions and Prepositions.

Note—Unlike English, the prepositions in Gujarati follow the noun; as—ઘરમાં, *ghur-mān*, in the house.

English	Gujarati	Gujarati (romanized)
About	આસપાસ	*āspās*
,, , nearly	આશરે	*āshre*
above	ઉપર	*oŏpur*
,, , more than	ઉપરાંત	*oŏprānt*
according to	પ્રમાણે	*prumāṇe*

English	Gujarati	Gujarati (romanize)
after	પછી, પાછળ	*puchee, pāchul*
afterwards	ત્યાર પછી	*tyār-puchee*
again	ફરીથી	*fureethee*
against	સામે	*sāme*
almost	લગભગ	*lugbhug*
also	વળી, પણ	*vulee, puṇ*
although	જોકે	*jo-ke*
altogether	તદ્દન	*tudun*
always	હમેશા	*humeshā*
and	અને, તથા	*une, tuthā*
as much as	જેટલું-તેટલું	*jetloon-tetloon*
at first	પહેલાં	*puhelān*
at last	આખરે	*ākhure*
at once	એકદમ	*ekdum*
at present	હાલ	*hāl*
because, for, since	કારણકે	*kāruṇ ke*
before (adv)	પહેલાં	*puhelāṇ*
„ (prep)	આગળ, પાસે	*āguḷ pāse*
behind	પાછળ	*pāchul*
below, beneath	નીચે, તળે	*neeche, tuḷe*
between	વચ્ચે	*vuch-che*
but	પણ	*puṇ*
down	નીચે	*neeche*
during	દરમિયાન	*durmiyān*
early	વહેલું	*vuheloon*
elsewhere	બીજે	*beeje*
except, without	સિવાય, વિના	*sivāy, vina*
far	દૂર	*door*
for (prep)	માટે, વાસ્તે	*māṭe, vāste*
hardly, scarcely	ભાગ્યેજ	*bhāgyej*
here	અહિં	*uhiṅ*
how	કેમ	*kem*

English	Gujarati	Gujarati (romanized)
however	તોપણ	*topuṇ*
if	જો-તો	*jo-to*
immediately, soon	તરત	*turut*
in, into	માં	*mān*
indeed, really	ખરેખર	*k̲k̲urek̲h̲ur*
inside, within	અંદર	*undur*
instead	બદલે	*budle*
just now, presently	હમણાં	*humṇān*
late	મોડું	*modŏŏn*
like	જેવું	*jevŏŏn*
much	ઘણું, બહુ	*g̲h̲uṇŏŏn, buhŏŏ*
near	પાસે, નજીક	*pase, nujik*
not	નહિ	*nuhi*
notwithstanding	છતાં	*c̲h̲utān*
now	હવે, હમણાં	*huve, humṇān*
of course	અલબત્ત	*ulbutt*
often	વારંવાર	*vārun-vār*
only	ફક્ત, માત્ર	*fukt, mātr*
or	અથવા,	*uthvā, ke*
otherwise	નહિતો	*nuhito*
out of	માંથી	*mānthee*
outside, without	બહાર	*buhār*
perhaps	કદાચ	*kudāch*
quickly, fast	જલદી	*juldee*
since	થયાં	*thuyān*
so	એમ, એવું	*em, evŏŏn*
sometimes	કોઇ કોઇ વાર	*koi-koi-vār*
suddenly	અચાનક, એકાએક	*uchānuk, ekā-ek*
that (conj)	કે	*ke*
then	પછી	*puc̲h̲ee*
thence	ત્યાંથી	*tyānthee*

English	Gujarati	Gujarati (romanized)
thenceforth	ત્યારથી	*tyārthee*
there	ત્યાં	*tyān*
thus	આ પ્રમાણે	*ā prumāṇe*
together	સાથે	*sāthe*
towards	તરફ	*turuf*
till, until	જ્યાંસુધી–ત્યાંસુધી	*jyān-soŏdhee-tyān-soŏdhee*
upon, on	ઉપર	*ŏŏpur*
well	વારૂ, ઠીક	*vārŏŏ, theek*
when	જ્યારે-ત્યારે	*jyāre-tyāre*
where	ક્યાં, જ્યાં–ત્યાં	*kyān; jyān-tyān*
why	શામાટે	*shā-māṭe*
with	સાથે	*sāthe*
yet (adv)	હજી	*hujee*
,, (conj)	તોપણ	*tapuṇ*

III. Outline of Grammar.

I. Arrangement of words in a Sentence.

In English—Subject, Verb, object, Adverb.
In Gujarati—Subject, object; Adverb, Verb.

Vocabulary.

Verbs (Imperative forms).	Adverbs and Conjunctions.
Go, જાઓ, *jā-o*	Here, અહિં, *uhin*
come, આવો, *āvo*	there, ત્યાં, *tyān*
stand, ઉભા રહો, *oobhā ruho*	fast, જલદી, *juldee*
sit, બેસો, *beso*	still, શાંત, *shānt*
run, દોડો, *dodo*	slowly, ધીમેથી, *dheemethee*
stop, અટકો, *utko*	back, પાછા, *pāchī*
speak, બોલો, *bolo*	and, અને, *une*
play, રમો, *rumo*	
stay, રહો, *ruho*	
talk, વાત કરો, *vāt kuro*	

Examples:—

English	Gujarati	Gujarati (romanized).
Come here	અહિં આવો	*uhin āvo*
Go there	ત્યાં જાઓ	*tyān jāo*
Come back	પાછા આવો	*pāchī āvo*
Go back	પાછા જાઓ	*pāchā jāo*
Sit here	અહિં બેસો	*uhin beso*
Speak slowly	ધીમેથી બોલો	*dheemethee bolo*
Run fast	જલદી દોડ	*juldee dodo*
Stay here	અહિં રહો	*uhin ruho*
Stop there	ત્યાં અટકો	*tyān utko*
Sit still	શાંત બેસો	*shānt beso*
Come here and talk.	અહિં આવો વાત કરો	*uhin āvo une vāt kuro*

II. Gender

(1) Masculine nouns generally end in ઓ (*o*) as in છોકરો, *chokro*, a boy.

(2) Feminine nouns generally end in ઈ (*ee*) as in છોકરી, *chokree*, a girl.

(3) Neuter nouns generally end in ઉં (*ŏŏn*) as in છોકરૂં, *chokrŏŏn*, a child.

Vocabulary.

Take, લો, *lo*
put, મૂકો, *mooko*
eat, ખાઓ, *khāo*
drink, પીઓ, *peeo*
bring, લાવો, *lāvo*
read, વાંચો, *vāncho*
hold, પકડો, *pukdo*
open, ઉઘાડો, *ŏŏghādo*
shut, બંધ કરો. *bundh kuro*
this, આ, *ā*

Milk, દૂધ, *doodh n.*
mango, કેરી, *keree f.*
water, પાણી, *pāṇee n.*
book, ચોપડી, *chopdee f.*
door, બારણું, *bārṇŏŏn n.*
cup, પ્યાલો, *pyālo m.*
tea, ચા, *chā f.*
box, પેટી, *petee f.*
now, હવે, *huve*
then, પછી, *puchee*

Examples:—

English	Gujarati	Gujarati (romanized)
Come here, then go back.	અહિં આવો, પછી પાછા જાઓ	*uhin āvo, puchee pāchā jāo*
Drink this water	આ પાણી પીઓ	*ā pāṇee peeo*
Read this book	આ ચોપડી વાંચો	*ā chopdee vāncho*
Eat this mango	આ કેરી ખાઓ	*ā keree khāo*
Shut the door	બારણું બંધ કરો	*bārṇŏŏn bundh kuro*
Open the door	બારણું ઉઘાડો	*bārṇŏŏn ŏŏghādo*
Drink this milk slowly.	આ દૂધ ધીમેથી પીઓ	*ā doodh dheemethee peeo*
Take this cup of tea.	ચાનો આ પ્યાલો લો	*chāno ā pyālo lo*
Hold this book	આ ચોપડી પકડો	*ā chopdee pukdo*
Bring the box here	પેટી અહિં લાવો	*petee uhin lāvo*

II Number.

The Plural of Nouns is generally formed by adding ઓ (*o*) as ચોપડીઓ, *chopḍee-o*, books.

Masculine nouns ending in ઓ (*o*) form their plural by changing ઓ (*o*) into આ (*ā*) as-ઘોડો, *g̲hoḍo*, a horse; ઘોડા, *g̲hoḍa*, horses.

Neuter nouns ending in ઉં (*ŏŏn*) form their plural by changing ઉં (*ŏŏn*) into આં (*ān*) as-ઈંડું, *inḍŏŏn*, an egg; ઈંડાં, *inḍān*, eggs.

Vocabulary.

windows, બારીઓ, *bāreeo f. p.*
do not, માં, *mān*
not, નહિ, *nuhi*

Examples:—

English	Gujarati	Gujarati (romanlz. l)
Do not come here	અહિં આવો માં	*uhin āvo mān*
Do not stand there	ત્યાં ઉભા રહો માં	*tyān ŏŏb̲h̲ā ruho mān*
Do not open the windows.	બારીઓ ઉઘાડો માં	*bāreeo ŏŏg̲h̲āḍo mān*
Run fast; not there	જલદી દોડો; ત્યાં નહિ	*juldee doḍo; tyān nuhi*
Do not sit there	ત્યાં બેસો માં	*tyān beso mān*
Come and sit here	આવો અને અહિં બેસો	*āvo une uhin beso*
Do not read the book.	ચોપડી વાંચો માં	*chopḍee vāncho mān*
Do not drink water	પાણી પીઓ માં	*pāṇee peeo mān*

IV. Case.

There are Seven Cases in Gujarati. The following are the case endings:—

Nominative none

Objective	none; or ને (*ne*) in case of living beings
Agent or instrument	એ (*e*)
Dative	ને (*ne*)
Ablative	થી (*thee*)
Possessive	નો, ની, નું ના, નાં, (*no, nee, nŏŏn, nā, nān*) according to the gender and number of the noun possessed
Locative	માં (*mān*) or એ (*e*)

Note—Masculine nouns ending in ઓ (*o*) and Neuter nouns ending in ઉં (*ŏŏn*) change ઓ (*o*) and ઉં (*ŏŏn*) into આ (*ā*) before taking the case endings as-છોકરો, *chokro*; છોકરાને, *chokrā-ne*, to the boy; ઘેટું, *gheṭŏŏn*, ઘેટાને, *gheṭā-ne*, to the lamb.

Declensions of ઘોડો, *ghoḍo*, a horse; and ઘેટું, *gheṭŏŏn*, a lamb

Nom. ઘોડો, *ghoḍo*, horse	ઘેટું, *gheṭŏŏn*, lamb
Obj. ઘોડો, ઘોડાને, *ghoḍo*, *ghoḍāne*, horse	ઘેટું, ઘેટાને, *gheṭŏŏn*, *gheṭāne*, lamb
Ag. ઘોડાએ, *ghoḍā-e*, horse	ઘેટાએ,, *gheṭā-e*, lamb
Dat. ઘોડાને, *ghoḍāne*, to the horse	ઘેટાને, *gheṭāne*, to the lamb
Abl. ઘોડાથી, *ghoḍāthee*, by the horse	ઘેટાથી, *gheṭāthee*, by the lamb
Poss. ઘોડાનો, *ghoḍāno* &c., of the horse	ઘેટાનું, *gheṭānŏŏn* &c., of the lamb
Loc. ઘોડામાં, *ghoḍāmān*, in the horse	ઘેટામાં, *gheṭāmān*, in the lamb

V. Personal Pronouns.

See Vocabulary, page 46.

Pronouns are inflected for case and are declinable for Number. There is, however, no distinction of Gender.

1st. Person, Masculine or Feminine.

Case.	Singular.	Plural.
Nom.	I, હું, *hoŏn*	we, અમે, *ume;* આપણે, *āpṇe*
Obj.	me, મને, *mune*	us, અમને, *umne;* આપણને, *āpuṇ-ne*
Ag.	I, મેં, *men*	we, અમે, *ume;* આપણે, *āpṇe*
Dat.	me, મને, *mune*	us, અમને, *umne;* આપણને, *āpuṇ-nc*
Abl.	by, from me, મારાથી, *mārāthee*	by, from us, અમારાથી, *umārāthee;* આપણાથી, *āpṇāthee*
Poss.	my, mine, મારો *māro* &c.	our, ours, અમારો, *umāro;* આપણો, *āpṇo* &c.
Loc.	in me, મારામાં, *mārāmān*	in us, અમારામાં, *umārāmān;* આપણામાં, *āpṇāmān*

2nd Person, Masculine or Feminine.

Case.	Singular.	Plural.
Nom.	Thou, તું, *toŏn*	you, તમે, *tume;* આપ, *āp*
Obj.	thee, તને, *tune*	you, તમને, *tumne;* આંપને, *āpne*
Ag.	thou, તેં, *ten*	you, તમે, *tume;* આપે, *āpe*
Dat.	thee, તને, *tune*	you, તમને, *tumne;* આપને, *āpne*
Abl.	by, from thee, તારાથી, *tārāthee*	by, from you, તમારાથી, *tumārāthee,* આપથી, *āpthee*
Poss.	thy, thine, તારૂં, *tāroŏn* &c.	your, yours, તમારૂં, *tumāroŏn;* આપનું, *āpnoŏn* &c.
Loc.	in thee, તારામાં, *tārāmān*	in you, તમારામાં, *tumārāmān;* આપનામાં, *āpṇāmān*

3rd Person, Masculine or Feminine.

Case.	Singular.	Plural.
Nom.	He, she, તે, *te*	They, તેઓ, *teo*
Obj.	him, her, તેને, *tene*	them, તેમને, *temne*
Ag.	he, she, તેણે, *teṇe*	they, તેમણે, *temṇe*
Dat.	him, her, તેને, *tene*	them, તેમને, *temne*
Abl.	by, from him, her, તેનાથી, *tenāthee*	by, from them, તેમનાથી, *temnāthee*
Poss	his, her, hers, તેનું, *tenoŏn* &c.	their, theirs, તેમનું, *temnoŏn* &c.
Loc.	in him, her, તેનામાં, *tenāmān*	in them, તેમનામાં, *temnāmān*

VI. Adjectives.

See Vocabulary, page 47

Some Adjectives undergo inflectional changes to agree with the Gender, Number and Case of the nouns they qualify; as—that horse, પેલો ઘોડો, *pelo g̲hodo*; that egg, પેલું ઇંડું, *peloŏn intoŏn.*

Adjectives ending in ઓ (*o*), ઇ (*i*) or ઉં (*oŏn*) are declinable; the rest are indeclinable; as—red horse, લાલ ઘોડો, *lāl g̲hoḍo*; red cloth લાલ કપડું, *lāl kupḍoŏn* &c.

Vocabulary

Small, નાનું, *nānoŏn d.*
large, મોટું, *motoŏn d.*
dirty, ગંદું, *gundoŏn d.*
ripe, પાકી, *pākee d.*
that, પેલું, *peloŏn d.*

glass, કાચ, *kāch m.*
piece, કટકો, *kutko m.*
to, ને, પાસે, માં, *ne, pāse, māin*
this, આ. *ā*

Examples:—

English	Gujarati	Gujarati (romanized)
Give me that book	પેલી ચોપડી મને આપો	*pelee chopḍee mune āpo*
Give this cup of milk to Magan	આ દૂધનો પ્યાલો મગનને આપો	*ā doodhno pyālo mugun-ne āpo*
Take that ripe mango	પેલી પાકી કેરી લો.	*pelee pākee keree lo*
Bring that piece of glass here	પેલો કાચનો કટકો અહિં લાવો	*pelo kāchno kuṭko uhin lāvo*
Do not drink that dirty water.	પેલું ગંદું પાણી પીઓ માં	*peloŏn gundoŏn pāṇee peeo māṅ*
Eat that small mango	પેલી નાની કેરી ખાઓ	*pelee nānee keree k̲hāo*
Open that large window	પેલી મોટી બારી ઉઘાડો	*pelee motee bāree oŏg̲hāḍo*

VII. Present Tense of 'to be'

I am, હું છું, *hoon choon*
Thou art, તું છે, *toon che*
He is, તે છે, *te che*
we are, અમે છીએ, *ume chee-e*
you are, તમે છો, *tume cho*
They are, તેઓ છે, *teo che*

Vocabulary.

what, શું, *shoon*
who, કોણ, *koṇ*
where, ક્યાં, *kyān*
yes, હા, *hā*
no, ના, *nā*
whose, કોનું *konoon d.*
sweet, મીઠી, *meethee d.*
sour, ખાટી, *khātee d.*
clever, હોશિયાર, *hoshiyār*
father, બાપ, *bāp m.*
mother, મા *mā f.*
brother, ભાઇ *bhāi m.*
sister, બહેન, *buhen f.*
man, માણસ, *māṇus m.*
name, નામ, *nām n.*
town, ગામ, *gām n.*
lazy, આળસુ, *āḷsoo*
but, પણ, *puṇ*
is not, નથી, *nuthee*

Examples:—

English	Gujarati	Gujarati (romanized)
What is this?	આ શું છે ?	*ā shoon che ?*
It is a cup of tea	તે ચાનો પ્યાલો છે	*te chāno pyālo che*
What is your name?	તમારૂં નામ શું છે ?	*tumāroon nām shoon che ?*
My name is Magan	મારૂં નામ મગન છે	*māroon nām Mugun che*
Tell me your brother's name.	તમારા ભાઇનું નામ મને કહો	*tumārā bhāi-noon nām mune kuho*
Who is that man?	પેલો માણસ કોણ છે?	*pelo māṇus koṇ che ?*
He is my father	તે મારો બાપ છે	*te māro bāp che*
Where is your sister?	તમારી બહેન ક્યાં છે ?	*tumāree buhen kyān che ?*
She is in the town	તે ગામમાં છે	*te gām-mān che*

English	Gujarati	Gujarati (romanized)
Where is your book ?	તમારી ચોપડી ક્યાં છે ?	*tumāree chopdee kyān che ?*
It is here	તે અહિં છે	*te uhin che*
Whose is this horse?	આ ઘોડો કોનો છે ?	*ā ghodo kono che ?*
It is not mine	તે મારો નથી	*te māro nuthee*
Is this his book?	આ ચોપડી તેની છે ?	*ā chopdee tenee che ?*
No, it is yours	ના, તે તમારી છે	*nā, te tumāree che*
These mangoes are not sweet.	આ કેરીઓ મીઠી નથી.	*ā kereeo meethee nuthee*
Bring those boxes of books here	પેલી ચોપડીઓની પેટીઓ અહિં લાવો	*pelee chopdeeo-nee petee-o uhin lāvo*
You are clever, but you are lazy	તમે હોશિયાર છો, પણ તમે આળસુ છો.	*tume hoshiyār cho, pun tume ālsoo cho*

VIII. The Present Tense.

See Vocabulary page 50

bolvoon બોલવું, to speak

I speak; am speaking†, હું બોલું છું. *hoon boloon choon*

We speak; are speaking. અમે બોલીએ છીએ, *ume bolee-e chee-e*

Thou speakest; art speaking, તું બોલે છે, *toon bole che*

You speak; are speaking, તમે બોલો છો, *tume bolo cho*

He speaks; is speaking, તે બોલે છે, *te bole che*

They speak; are speaking, તેઓ બોલે છે, *teo bole che*

juvoon, જવું, *to go*

I am to go, હું જવાનો છું, *hoon juvāno choon*

We are to go, અમે જવાના છીએ, *ume juvānā chee-e*

Thou art to go, તું જવાનો છે, *toon juvāno che*

You are to go, તમે જવાના છો, *tume juvānā cho*

He is to go, તે જવાનો છે, *te juvāno che*

They are to go, તેઓ જવાના છે. *teo juvānā che*

† There is only one form for the Present Imperfect and Present Indefinite in Gujarati.

Vocabulary.

walk, ચાલવું, *chālvoŏn*
sing, ગાવું, *gāvoŏn*
jump, કૂદવું, *koodvoŏn*
bark, ભસવું, *bhusvoŏn*
talk, વાત કરવી, *vāt kurvee*
fly, ઉડવું, *oŏḍvoŏn*
cry, રડવુ *ruḍvoŏn*
write, લખવું *lukhoŏn*
one, એક. *ek*
two, બે, *be*
three, ત્રણ, *truṇ*
daily, રોજ, *roj*
An old man, ડોસો, *ḍoso m.*
an old woman, ડોસી, *ḍosee f.*
eye, આંખ, *ānkh f.*
ink, શાહી, *shāhee f,*
do not, does not, નથી, *nuthee*
bite, કરડવું, *kurudvoŏn*

song, ગીત, *geet n.*
woman, બાઇડી, *bā-i-ḍee f.*
cat, બિલાડી, *bilāḷee f.*
air, હવા, *huvā f.*
child, છોકરૂં, *chokroŏn n.*
letter, કાગળ. *kāguḷ m.*
rice, ચોખા, *chokhā m. p.*
dog, કુતરો, *kootro m.*
bird પક્ષી *pukshee n.*
cricket, ક્રિકેટ, *kriket n.*
very, બહુ, *buhoŏ*
school, નિશાળ, *nishaḷ f.*
a few, થોડા, *thoḍa d.*
white, ધોળો, *dhoḷo d.*
red, રાતો, *rāto d.*
black, કાળો *kāḷo d.*
big, મોટો, *moṭo d.*
good, સારો, ભલો, *sāro, bhulo d.*

English	Gujarati	Gujarati (romanized)
My little brother goes to school daily.	મારો નાનો ભાઇ રોજ નિશાળે જાય છે	*māro nāno bhāi roj nishāḷe jāy che*
The boys are eating mangoes	છોકરા કેરીઓ ખાય છે.	*chokrā keree-o khāy che*
Girls are singing songs.	છોકરીઓ ગીતો ગાય છે	*chokree-o geeto gāy che*
I am writing a letter.	હું કાગળ લખું છું	*hoŏn kāguḷ lukhoŏn choŏn*
Those little boys are playing cricket.	પેલા નાના છોકરા ક્રિકેટ રમે છે	*pelā nānā chokrā kriket rume che*

English	Gujarati	Gujarati (romanized)
They are eating rice and milk.	તેઓ દૂધ ચોખા ખાય છે	*teo doodh chokhā khāy che*
Those three women are talking.	પેલી ત્રણ બાઇડીઓ વાત કરે છે	*pelee trun bā-i-deeo vāt kure che*
Magan is reading and writing.	મગન વાંચે છે અને લખે છે	*mugun vānche che une lukhe che*
You are writing a letter to your father.	તમેં તમારા બાપને કાગળ લખો છો	*tume tumārā bāpne kāgul lukho cho*
Her little child is playing.	તેનું નાનું છોકરૂં રમે છે.	*tenŏŏn nānŏŏn chorŏŏn rume che*
That old woman is very good.	પેલી ડોસી બહુ ભલી છે	*pelee ḍosee buhŏŏ bhulee che*
This old man does not walk fast.	આ ડોસો જલદી ચાલતો નથી	*ā ḍoso juldee chālto nuthee*
Your eyes are red	તમારી આંખો રાતી છે.	*tumāree ānkho rātee che*
My big dog does not bite.	મારો મોટો કૂતરો કરડતો નથી	*māro moto kootro kuruḍto nuthee*
Give me a few rupees.	મને થોડા રૂપિયા આપો	*mune thoḍā rŏŏpiyā āpo*

IX. To have.

I have, મારી પાસે છે, *māree pāse che*; મારે છે, *māre che*
We have, અમારી પાસે છે, *umāree pāse che*; અમારે છે, *umāre che*
Thou hast, તારી પાસે છે, *tāree pāse che*; તારે છે, *tāre che*
You have, તમારી પાસે છે, *tumāree pāse che*; તમારે છે, *tumāre che*
He has, તેની પાસે છે, *tenee pāse che*; તેને છે, *tene che*
They have, તેમની પાસે છે, *temnee pāse che*, તેમને છે, *temne che*

Vocabulary.

Son, દીકરો, *deekro m.* — how many, કેટલા, *ketlā d.*
tank, તળાવ, *tulāv n.* — how much, કેટલું, *ketlŏŏn d.*

business, કામ, *kām n.*
frog, દેડકું, *deḍkoon n.*
pencil, સિસાપેન, *sisāpen f.*
watch, ઘડિયાળ, *ghuḍiyāḷ n.*
four, ચાર, *chār*
long, લાંબું, *lānboon*
nice, સુંદર, *soondur*
feet, પગ, *pug*

Examples:—

English	Gujarati	Gujarati (romanized)
My brother has a nice dog.	મારા ભાઇ પાસે સુંદર કૂતરો છે	*mārā bhāi pāse soondur kootro che*
You have a good pen.	તમારી પાસે સારી કલમ છે	*tumāree pāse sāree kulum che*
He has my books	તેની પાસે મારી ચોપડીઓ છે	*tenee pāse māree chopḍee-o che*
That old woman has two sons.	પેલી ડોસીને બે દીકરા છે	*pelee ḍosee-ne be deekrā che*
I have much business.	મારે ઘણું કામ છે	*māre ghuṇoon kām che*
You have a nice watch.	તમારે સુંદર ઘડિયાળ છે	*tumāre soondur ghuḍiyāḷ che*
There are many frogs in this tank.	આ તળાવમાં ઘણાં દેડકાં છે	*ā tuḷāv-māṅ ghu-ṇāṅ deḍkāṅ che*
How many brothers and sisters have you?	તમારે કેટલાં ભાઇ બહેન છે ?	*tumāre ketlāṅ hāi buhen che?*
How much milk does your cow give?	તમારી ગાય કેટલું દૂધ આપે છે ?	*tumāree gāy ket-loon doodh āpe che?*

X The Past Tense.

See Vocabulary page 50

(1) An intransitive verb agrees with the *subject* in Gender and Number.

(2) A transitive verb generally agrees with the *object* in Gender and Number.

(3) In a transitive verb, the subject is placed in the 3rd (Agent) case.

Intransitive verb-to go, જવું, *juvoon*; ગયો, *guyo*, went.

I went, હું ગયો, *hoon guyo* We went, અમે ગયા, *ume guyā*

Thou went, તું ગયો, *toon guyo* You went, તમે ગયા, *tume guyā*

He went, તે ગયો, *te guyo* They went, તેઓ ગયા, *teo guyā*

Transitive verb-to eat, ખાવું, *khāvoon*, ખાધું *khādhoon*, ate.

I ate a mango, મેં કેરી ખાધી, *mein keree khādhee*

We ate a mango, અમે કેરી ખાધી, *ume keree khādhee*

Thou ate a mango, તેં કેરી ખાધી, *tein keree khādhee*

You ate a mango, તમે કેરી ખાધી, *tume keree khādhee*

He ate a mango, તેણે કેરી ખાધી, *tene keree khādhee*

They ate a mango, તેમણે કેરી ખાધી, *temne keree khādhee*

Vocabulary.

Hour, કલાક, *kulāk m.*
carpenter, સુતાર, *sootār m.*
boat, હોડી *hodee f.*
chair, ખુરસી, *khoorsee f.*
morning, સવાર, *suvār f.*
tiger, વાઘ, *vāgh m.*
Englishman, અંગ્રેજ, *ungrej*
show, બતાવવું, *butāv-voon*
count, ગણવું, *gunvoon*
kill, મારવું, *mārvoon*
new, નવા, *nuvee*
for, માટે, વાસ્તે, *māte, vāste*
five, પાંચ, *pānch*
laugh, હસવું, *husvoon*
make, બનાવવું, *bunāv-voon*

Examples:—

English	Gujarati	Gujarati (romanized)
Boys ran	છોકરા દોડયા	*chokrā dodyā*
Magan played five hours.	મગન પાંચ કલાક રમ્યો	*mugun pānch kulāk rumyo*
They walked slowly.	તેઓ ધીમેથી ચાલ્યા	*teo dheemethee chālyā*
Cats drank milk	બિલાડીઓએ દૂધ પીધું	*bilādee-o-e doodh peedhoon*

English	Gujarati	Gujarati (romanized)
This Englishman killed many tigers.	આ અંગ્રેજે ઘણા વાઘ માર્યા	*ā ungreje ghuṇā vāgh māryā*
The girl laughed	છોકરી હસી	*chokree husee*
He showed me his new book.	તેણે મને તેની નવી ચોપડી બતાવી	*teṇe mune tenee nuvee chopḍee butāvee*
The carpenter made two chairs for me.	સુતારે મારે માટે બે ખુરસી બનાવી	*sootāre māre māṭe be khoorsee bunāvee*
I wrote three letters this morning.	આજ સવારે મેં ત્રણ કાગળ લખ્યા	*āj suvāre men truṇ kāguḷ lukhyā*
Did you take tea?	તમે ચા પીધી ?	*tume chā peedhee?*
No. I took milk	ના. મેં દૂધ પીધું	*nā. men doodh peedhoon*
Did you count all the boys?	તમે બધા છોકરા ગણ્યા?	*tume budhā chokrā guṇyā ?*
Did he see the new boat?	તેણે નવી હોડી જોઇ ?	*teṇe nuvee hoḍee jo-i ?*
Where did he go?	તે ક્યાં ગયો ?	*te kyān guyo ?*

XI. Was; Had.

I was, હું હતો, *hoon huto*; We were, અમે હતા, *ume hutā*

Thou wast, તું હતો, *toon huto*; You were, તમે હતા, *tume hutā*

He was, તે હતો, *te huto* They were, તેઓ હતા, *teo hutā*

I had, મારી પાસે હતું, *māree pāse hutoon*; મારે હતું *māre hutoon*

We had, અમારી પાસે હતું, *umāree pāse hutoon*; અમારે હતું. *umāre hutoon*

Thou hadst, તારી પાસે હતું, *tāree pāse hutoon*; તારે હતું, *tāre hutoon*

You had, તમારી પાસે હતું, *tumāree pāse hutoon*; તમારે હતું, *tumāre hutoon*

He had, તેની પાસે હતું, *tenee pāse hutoon;* તેને હતું, *tene hutoon*
They had, તેમની પાસે હતું *temnee pāse hutoon;* તેમને હતું, *temne hutoon*

Vocabulary.

Shepherd, ભરવાડ, *bhurvād m.*
daughter, દીકરી, *deekree f.*
road, રસ્તો, *rusto m.*
lamb, ઘેટું, *ghetoon n.*
buffalo, ભેંસ, *bhens f.*
empty, ખાલી, *khālee ind.*
ill, માંદા, *māndā d.*
seven, સાત, *sāt*
yesterday, ગઇ કાલ, *gui kāl f.*
fruit, ફળ, *ful n.*
cow, ગાય, *gāy f.*
basket, ટોપલી, *toplee f.*
flower, ફુલ, *fool n.*
angry, ગુસ્સે, *goosse*
narrow, સાંકડો, *sānklo d.*
with, સાથે, *sāthe*
hand, હાથ, *hāth m.*

Examples:—

English	Gujarati	Gujarati (romanized)
Were you ill yesterday?	ગઇ કાલે તમે માંદા હતા?	*gui kāle tume māndā hutā ?*
We had seven books.	અમારી પાસે સાત ચોપડીઓ હતી	*umāree pāse sāt chopdee-o hutee*
That shepherd has many lambs.	પેલા ભરવાડ પાસે ઘણાં ઘેટાં છે	*pelā bhurvād pāse ghunān ghetān che*
She was angry with me.	તે મારી સાથે ગુસ્સે હતી	*te māree sāthe goosse hutee*
My father had a black horse.	મારા બાપ પાસે કાળો ઘોડો હતો	*mārā bāp pāse kālo ghodo huto*
She had a basket of flowers in her hand.	તેના હાથમા ફુલની ટોપલી હતી	*tenā hāthmān fool-nee toplee hutee*
How many sons and daughters have you?	તમારે કેટલા દીકરા દીકરીઓ છે ?	*tumāre ketlā deekrā deekree-o che?*
The roads were very narrow.	રસ્તા ઘણા સાંકડા હતા	*rustā ghunā sānkdā hutā.*

English	Gujarati	Gujarati (romanized)
I had two cows and one buffalo	મારે બે ગાયો અને એક ભેંસ હતી	māre be gāyo une ek bhen· hutee
What was his father's name ?	તેના બાપનું નામ શું હતું ?	tenā bāpnoon nān shoon hutoon"

XII. The Past Imperfect Tense.

See Vocabulary, page 50

I was going, હું જતો હતો, *hoon juto huto*
We were going, અમે જતા હતા, *ume jutā hutā*
Thou wast going, તું જતો હતો, *toon juto huto*
You were going, તમે જતા હતા, *tume jutā hutā*
He was going, તે જતો હતો, *te juto huto*
They were going, તેઓ જતા હતા, *teo jutā hutā*

Vocabulary.

Lesson, પાઠ, *pāṭh n.*
carriage, ગાડી, *gāḍee f.*
clerk કારકુન, *kārkoon m.*
fiddle, ફિડલ, *fiḍul f.*
office, ઑફિસ, *ofis f.*
home, ઘર, *ghur n.*
when, જ્યારે-ત્યારે, *jyāre-tyāre.*
see, મળવું, *muḷvoon*
call, બોલાવવું, *bolāv-voon*
play on, વગાડવું, *vugāḍvoon*
behind, પાછળ, *pāchuḷ*
out, બહાર, *buhār*

Examples:—.

English	Gujarati	Gujarati (romanized
I was reading my lessons when you came.	તમે આવ્યા ત્યારે હું મારા પાઠ વાંચતો હતો	tume āvyā tyāre hoon mārā pāṭh vānchto huto
He was writing a letter when I called him.	મેં તેને બોલાવ્યો ત્યારે તે કાગળ લખતો હતો	men tene bolāvyo tyāre te kāguḷ lukhto huto
The clerks were talking when I went to the office	હું ઓફિસે ગયો ત્યારે કારકુનો વાત કરતા હતા	hoon ofise guyo tyāre kārkoono vāt kurtā hutā

English	Gujarati	Gujarati (romanized)
He was singing and his sister was playing on the fiddle.	તે ગાતો હતો અને તેની બહેન ફિડલ વગાડતી હતી	*te gāto huto une tenee buhen fiḍul vugāḍtee hutee*
When I was going home, I saw him in a carriage.	હું ઘેર જતો હતો ત્યારે મેં તેને ગાડીમાં જોયો	*hoŏn gher juto huto tyīre mein tene gāḍeemān joyo*
He was going out when I went to see him this morning.	આજ સવારે હું તેને મળવા ગયો ત્યારે તે બહાર જતો હતો	*āj suvāre hoŏn tene mulvā guyo tyāre te buhār juto huto*
They were walking behind us.	તેઓ અમારી પાછળ ચાલતા હતા	*teo umāree pāchul chāltā hutā*

XIII. The Future Tense.

I shall go, હું જઇશ, *hoŏn juish*; We shall go, અમે જઇશું, *ume juishoŏn*

Thou wilt go, તું જઇશ, *toŏn juish*; You will go, તમે જશો, *tume jusho*

He will go, તે જશે, *te jushe*; They will go, તેઓ જશે, *teo jushe*

Vocabulary.

Spring. વસંત, *vusunt f.*
peon, પટાવાળો, *puṭāvāḷo m.*
room, ઓરડો, *orḍo* m.
work, કામ, *kām n.*
month, મહિનો, *muhino m.*
sugar, ખાંડ, *khānḍ f.*
twelve, બાર, *bār*
o'clock, વાગતાં, *vāgtān*
today, આજે *āje*
tomorrow. કાલ, *kāl*
some, થોડાક, *thoḍāk*
begin, શરૂ થવું, *shuroŏ thuvoŏn*
blossom, ખીલવું, *kheelvoŏn*

Examples:—

English	Gujarati	Gujarati (romanized)
I will give you some books tomoorow.	કાલે હું તમને થોડીક ચોપડીઓ આપીશ	*kāle hoŏn tumne thoḍeek chopḍee-o āpeesh*
He will go to England in the month of March.	તે માર્ચ મહિનામાં ઇંગ્લાંડ જશે	*te mārch muhinā-mān inglānḍ jushe*
The work will begin at twelve o'clock.	બાર વાગતાં કામ શરૂ થશે	*bār vāgtōn kām shuroŏ thushe*
The flowers will blossom in the spring.	વસંતમાં ફુલ ખીલશે	*vus ntmān foŏl k͟heelshe*
Will you take tea?	તમે ચા પીશો ?	*tume chā peesho?*
She will give you milk and sugar.	તે તમને દૂધ અને ખાંડ આપશે	*te tumne doodh une k͟hānḍ āpshe*
Go to my room, the peon will open the door.	મારા ઓરડામાં જાઓ, પટાવાળો બારણું ઉઘાડશે	*mārā orḍā-mān jā o, puṭāvāḷo bārṇoŏn oŏg͟hāḍ-she*
He will come today.	તે આજે આવશે	*te āje āvushe*

XIV. The Present Perfect Tense.

See Vocabulary page 50

I have eaten, મેં ખાધું છે, *men k͟hādhoŏn che*
We have eaten, અમે ખાધું છે, *ume k͟hādhoŏn c͟he*
Thou hast eaten, તેં ખાધું છે, *ten k͟hādhoŏn c͟he*
You have eaten, તમે ખાધું છે, *tume k͟hādhoŏn c͟he*
He has eaten, તેણે ખાધું છે, *teṇe k͟hādhoŏn c͟he*
They have eaten, તેમણે ખાધું છે, *temṇe k͟hādhoŏn c͟he*

The Pluperfect Tense.

I had eaten, મેં ખાધું હતું, *men k͟hādhoŏn hutoŏn*

We had eaten, અમે ખાધું હતું, *ume khādhoon hutoon*
Thou hadst eaten, તેં ખાધું હતું, *ten khādhoon hutoon*
You had eaten, તમે ખાધું હતું, *tume khādhoon hutoon*
He had eaten, તેણે ખાધું હતું, *tene khādhoon hutoon*
They had eaten, તેમણે ખાધું હતું, *temne khādhoon hutoon*

Note:—In both these tenses (as in the Past Tense) the Verb, if transitive, agrees with the *object* in Gender, and Number, and the subject takes the 3rd (agent) case ending.

Vocabulary.

Doctor, વૈદ્ય, *Vaidy m.*
police, સિપાઇ, *sipāi m.*
patient, દરદી *durdee m.*
finger, આંગળી, *ānglee f.*
thief, ચોર, *chor m.*
ring, વીંટી, *veentee f.*
elephant, હાથી, *hāthee m.*
prize, ઇનામ, *inām n.*
before, પહેલાં, *puhelān*
to work, મહેનત કરવી, *mehenut kurvee*
to copy, નકલ કરવી, *nukul kurvee*
to finish, પૂરું કરવું, *pooroon kurvoon*
to lose, ખોવું, *khovoon*
to die, મરી જવું, *muree juvoon*
to run away, નાસી જવું, *nāsee juvoon*
because, કારણકે, *kārunke*
hard, સખત, *sukhut*
ever, કદિ, *kudi*

Examples:—

English	Gujarati	Gujarati (romanized)
I have lost my ring	મેં મારી વીંટી ખોઇ છે	*mein māree veentee khoi che*
The peon has shut the window.	પટાવાળાએ બારી બંધ કરી છે	*putāvālāe bāree bundh kuree che*
My sister has cut her finger	મારી બહેને પોતાની આંગળી કાપી છે	*māree buhene potānee ānglee kāpee che*

English	Gujarati	Gujarati (romanized)
The thief had run away before the police came.	સિપાઇ આવ્યા પહેલાં ચોર નાસી ગયો હતો	*sipāi āvyā puhelān chor nāsee guyo huto*
He had finished the work before I went.	હું ગયો તે પહેલાં તેણે કામ પૂરૂં કર્યું હતું	*hoŏn guyo te puhelān tene kām poorŏŏn kuryoŏn hutoŏn*
He got a prize, because he had worked hard.	તેને ઇનામ મળ્યું, કારણ કે તેણે સખત મહેનત કરી હતી	*tene inām mulyoŏn, kārunke tene sukhut muhenut kuree hutee.*
The patient had died before the doctor came.	વૈદ્ય આવ્યા પહેલા રદી મરી ગયો હતો	*vaidy āvyā puhelān durdee muree guyo huto*
Have you brought the letter ? No. my brother will send it tomorrow	તમે કાગળ લાવ્યા છો ? નાં. મારો ભાઇ તે કાલે મોકલશે	*tume kāgul lāvyā cho ? nā. māro bhāi te kāle mokulshe*
Has the clerk copied the letter?	કારકુને કાગળની નકલ કરી છે ?	*kārkoone kāgulnee nukul kuree che ?*
Have you ever seen an elephant?	તમે કદિ હાથી જોયો છે?	*tume kudi hāthee joyo che ?*
I had been to his house yesterday	કાલે હું તેને ઘેર ગયો હતો	*kāle hoŏn tene gher guyo huto*

XV. Can, May, Must, Should, Ought to.

See Vocabulary page 50

I can speak, હું બોલી શકું છું, *hoŏn bolee shukoŏn choŏn*
We can speak, અમે બોલી શકીએ છીએ, *ume bolee shukee-e chee-e*
Thou canst speak, તું બોલી શકે છે, *toŏn bole shuke che*
You can speak, તમે બોલી શકો છો, *tume bolee shuko cho*
He can speak, તે બોલી શકે છે, *te bolee shuke che*
They can speak, તેઓ બોલી શકે છે, *teo bolee shuke che*

May.

I may go, હું જાઉં, *hoon jāoon*; We may go, અમે જઇએ, *ume jui-e*

Thou mayest go, તું જાય, *toon jāy*; You may go, તમે જાઓ, *tume jā-o*

He may go, તે જાય, *te jāy*; They may go, તેઓ જાય, *teo jāy*

Must, should, ought to, જોઇએ, *jo-i-e.*

I must (should, ought to) go, મારે જવું જોઇએ, *māre juvoon jo-i-e*

We must (should, ought to) go, અમારે જવું જોઇએ, *umāre juvoon jo-i-e*

Thou must (should, ought to) go, તારે જવું જોઇએ, *tāre juvoon jo-i-e*

You must (should, ought to) go, તમારે જવું જોઇએ, *tumāre juvoon jo-i-e*

He must (should, ought to) go, તેણે જવું જોઇએ, *tene juvoon jo-i-e*

They must (should, ought to) go, તેમણે જવું જોઇએ, *temne juvoon jo-i-e*

I must have gone, હું ગયો હઇશ, *hoon guyo huish*

We must have gone, અમે ગયા હઇશું, *ume guyā huishoon*

Thou must have gone, તું ગયો હઇશ, *toon guyo huish*

You must have gone, તમે ગયા હશો, *tume guyā husho*

He must have gone, તે ગયો હશે, *te guyo hushe*

They must have gone, તેઓ ગયા હશે, *teo guyā hushe*

Vocabulary.

English, અંગ્રેજી, *ungrejee*; town, ગામ, *gām n.*

students, વિદ્યાર્થીઓ, *vidyārthee-o m. p.*

to be prepared, તૈયાર રહેવું, *taiyār ruhevoon*

beforehand, પહેલાંથી, *puhelānthee*

early, વહેલાં, *vuhelān*; to get up, ઉઠવું, *oothvoon*

to injure, ઇજા કરવી, *ijā kurvee*; any one, કોઇ, *koi*

station, સ્ટેશન, *steshun (E)*

to reach, પહોંચવું, *puhonchvoon*

English	Gujarati	Gujarati (romanized)
Can you speak English ?	તમે અંગ્રેજી બોલી શકો છો ?	*tume ungrejee bolee skuko cho ?*
It is five o'clock; you may go now	પાંચ વાગ્યા છે; હવે તમે જાઓ	*pānch vāgyā che; huve tume jā-o*
Can you not read this letter ?	તમે આ કાગળ વાંચી શકતા નથી ?	*tume ā kāgul vānchee shuktā nuthee ?*
May I go into the town ?	હું ગામમાં જાઉં ?	*hoon gām-mān jā-oon ?*
You must not eat too much.	તમારે બહુ ખાવું ન જોઇએ	*tumāre buhoo khāvoon nu jo-i-e*
He must work hard	તેણે સખત કામ કરવું જોઇએ	*tene sukhut kām kurvoon jo-i-e*
We should be prepared beforehand.	આપણે પહેલાંથી તૈયાર રહેવું જોઇએ	*āpne puhelānthee taiyār ruhevoon jo-i-e*
Students should get up early in the morning.	વિદ્યાર્થીઓએ સવારમાં વહેલાં ઉઠવું જોઇએ	*vidyārthee-o-e suvārmān vuhelān oothvoon jo-i-e*
We should not injure anyone.	આપણે કોઇને ઇજા કરવી ન જોઇએ	*āpne koine ijā kurvee nu jo-i-e*
He must have reached the station.	તે સ્ટેશને પહોંચ્યો હશે	*te steshune puhonchyo hushe*
You ought to have come earlier.	તમારે વહેલાં આવવું જોઇતું હતું	*tumāre vuhelān āvuvoon joitoon hutoon*
You must copy this letter before you go.	જતાં પહેલાં તમારે આ કાગળની નકલ કરવી જોઇએ	*jutān puhelān tumāre ā kāgulnee nukul kurvee jo-i-e*
They ought to have finished their work.	તેમણે પોતાનું કામ પૂરું કરવું જોઇતું હતું	*temne potānoon kām pooroon kurvoon joitoon hutoon*

IV. Conversational Phrases and Sentences

Greetings and Polite Expressions.

English	Gujarati	Gujarati (romanized
Good morning	(*Hindu*) રામરામ (*Mus*) સલામ	*rām-rām; sulām*
You are welcome	ભલે પધાર્યા	*bhule pudhāryā*
How do you do?	કેમ છો ?	*kem cho ?*
Quite well	ઠીક છે	*theek che*
Where do youcome from ?	ક્યાંથી આવો છો ?	*kyānthee āvo cho ?*
What is your name ?	તમારૂં નામ શું ?	*tumāroon nām shoon*
What is your age ?	તમારી ઉમર કેટલી છે ?	*tumāree oomur ketlee che ?*
What are you ?	તમે શું ધંધો કરો છો ?	*tume shoon dhundho kuro che ?*
How many children have you ?	તમારે શું છોકરાં છે ?	*tumāre shoon chokrān che ?*
What are you by caste ?	તમે નાતે કેવા છો ?	*tume nāte kevā cho.*
How far have you studied ?	તમે અભ્યાસ ક્યાં સુધી કર્યો છે ?	*tume ubhyās kyān soodhee kuryo che ?*
What has brought you here ?	અહિં શું કામે આવ્યા છો ?	*uhin shoon kāme āvyā cho ?*
Take a chair	ખુરસી ઉપર બેસો	*khoorsee oopur beso*
Are all well at home ?	ઘેર સૌ ખુશીમાં છે ?	*gher sow khoosheemān che?*
May I take leave?	રજા લઉં ?	*rujā luoon ?*
Why so much haste ?	એટલી બધી શું ઉતાવળ છે ?	*etlee badhee shoon ootāvul che ?*
I have some busi-	મારે થોડું કામ છે	*māre thodoon kām che*

English	Gujarati	Gujarati (romanized)
Sit down, let us talk	જરા બેસો, આપણે વાતો કરીએ	*jurā beso, āpṇe vāto kuree-e*
It is time to go to the office	ઑફિસે જવાનો વખત થયો છે	*ofise juvāno vukhut thuyo che*
There is plenty of time	હજી ઘણો વખત છે	*hujee ghuṇo vukhut che*
I must go at once	મારે જલદી જવાની જરૂર છે	*māre juldee juvānee juroor che*
When will you come again ?	ફરી કયારે આવશો ?	*furee kyāre āvsho ?*
I will come to-morrow morning	કાલ સવારે આવીશ	*kāl suvāre āveesh*
Do not fail to come	જરૂર આવજો	*juroor āvjo*
My house is a long way off	મારું ઘર ઘણું દૂર છે	*māroon ghur ghuṇoon door che*
Good-bye	પધારજો	*pudhārjo*

The Study of Gujarati.

English	Gujarati	Gujarati (romanized)
Can you read Gujarati ?	તમે ગુજરાતી વાંચી શકો છો ?	*tume goojrātee vānchee shuko cho ?*
Yes. I can read, but I can not speak it	હા. હું વાંચી શકું છું, પણ બોલી શકતો નથી	*hā. hoon vānchee shukoon choon, puṇ bolee shukto nuthee*
Talk to your servants in Gujarati	નોકરો સાથે ગુજરાતીમાં વાત કરો	*nokuro sāthe goojrātee-mān vāt kuro*
Mark their pronunciation	તેમના ઉચ્ચાર ઉપર ધ્યાન આપો	*temnā ooch-chār oopur dhyān āpo*
You should not put accent on Gujarati words	ગુજરાતી શબ્દો ઉપર ભાર મૂકવાનો નથી	*goojrātee shubdo oopur bhār mookvāno nuthee*
It requires a long practice	લાંબા મહાવરાની જરૂર છે	*lāmbā muhāvurānee juroor che*

English	Gujarati	Gujarati (romanized)
When did you begin the study ?	તમે અભ્યાસ ક્યારે શરૂ કર્યો ?	*tume ubhyās kyāre shurŏŏ kuryo?*
I have been studying it for the last six months	હું છ મહિના થયાં અભ્યાસ કરૂં છું	*hŏŏn chu muhinā thuyān ubhyās kurŏŏn chŏŏn*
Can you read a letter in Gujarati?	તમે ગુજરાતીમાં કાગળ વાંચી શકો છો ?	*tume gŏŏjrātee-mān kāguḷ vānchee shuko cho ?*
Yes. I can write a letter in Gujarati	હા. હું ગુજરાતીમાં કાગળ લખી શકું છું	*hā. hŏŏn gŏŏjrātee-mān kāguḷ lukhee shukŏŏn chŏŏn*
Open your book, and read page 7	ચોપડી ઉઘાડો અને સાતમું પાનું વાંચો	*chopḍee ŏŏghāḍo une sātmŏŏn pānŏŏn vāncho*
Your pronunciation is not quite correct	તમારા ઉચ્ચાર તદન સાચા નથી	*tumārā ŏŏch-chār tudun sāchā nuthee*
You must hear the natives speak the language	તમારે દેશીઓને તે ભાષા બોલતાં સાંભળવા જોઇએ	*tumāre deshee-o-ne te bhāshā boltān sānbhuḷvā jo-i-e*
Are you preparing for any examination ?	તમે કોઇ પરીક્ષાને માટે તૈયારી કરો છો ?	*tume ko-i pureekshāne māte taiyāree kuro cho ?*
You should devote some time to conversation.	તમારે વાતચિતમાં થોડો વખત ગાળવો જોઇએ	*tumāre vāt-chit-mān thoḍo vukh gāḷvo jo-i-e*
Translate these two pages into Gujarati.	આ બે પાનાંનો ગુજરાતીમાં તરજુમો કરો	*ā be pānān-no gŏŏj-rātee-mān tur-jŏŏmo kuro*

Useful and Necessary Expressions.

Bring a rupee-worth of sugar	એક રૂપિયાની ખાંડ લાવો	*ek rŏŏpiyānee khānḍ lāvo*

English	Gujarati	Gujarati (romanized)
To-morrow is a holiday	કાલે રજા છે	*kāle rujā che*
Go if you like	મરજી હોય તો જાઓ	*murjee hoy to jā-o*
He committed suicide	તેણે આપઘાત કર્યો	*teṇe āpghāt kuryo*
It is time to start	જવાનો વખત થયો છે	*juvāno vukhut thuyo che*
It is none of your business	તે તમારૂં કામ નથી	*te tumāroŏn kām nuthee*
Send it to Mr. Smith with my compliments	તે સ્મિથ સાહેબને મારા સલામ સાથે મોકલો	*te smith sāhebne mārā sulām sāthe moklo*
It depends on my getting leave	મને રજા મળવા ઉપર આધાર છે	*mune rujā muḷvā oŏpur ādhār che*
What did you ask?	તમે શું પૂછ્યું ?	*tume shoŏn poochyoŏn ?*
What is to be done now ?	હવે શું કરવું ?	*huve shoŏn kurvoŏn?*
Do you think it will rain ?	તમે ધારો છો કે વરસાદ થશે ?	*tume dhāro cho ke vursād thushe?*
What is the news?	શા ખબર છે ?	*shā khubur che ?*
I am feverish	મને તાવ આવ્યો છે	*mune tāv āvyo che*
I am unwell.	મને ઠીક નથી	*mune theek nuthee*
I have head-ache	મારૂં માથું દુખે છે	*māroŏn māthoŏn doŏkhe che*
I am tired	હું થાકી ગયો છું	*hoŏn thākee guyo choŏn*
I am sorry to hear it	એ સાંભળીને મને અફસોસ થાય છે	*e sānbhḷee-ne mune ufsos thāy che*
I feel sleepy	મને ઉંઘ આવે છે	*mune oŏngh āve che*
He was very angry with me	તે મારા ઉપર બહુ ગુસ્સે થયો	*te mārā oŏpur buhoŏ goŏsse thuyo*

English	Gujarati	Gujarati (romanized)
I know him well	હું તેને સારી પેઠે ઓળખું છું	*hoŏn tene sāree pethe olkhoŏn choŏn*
I was surprised to see it	તે જોઇને મને નવાઇ લાગી	*te jo-i-ne mune nuvāi lāgee*
The thief has stolen my watch	ચોર મારૂં ઘડિયાળ ચોરી ગયો છે	*chor māroŏn ghudiyāl choree guyo che*
I shall keep your advice in mind	હું તમારી શિખામણ યાદ રાખીશ	*hoŏn tumāree shikhāmun yād rākheesh*
I cannot call to mind any other example	મને બીજો કોઇ દાખલો યાદ આવતો નથી	*mune beejo ko-i dākhlo yād āvto nuthee*
This book will be of service to many	આ ચોપડી ઘણાને કામ લાગશે	*ā chopdee ghunāne kām lāgshe*
The children have been put to bed	છોકરાને સુવાડી દીધાં છે	*chokrān-ne soŏvādee deedhān che*
Let him take the business in hand at once	તેને કામ જલદી શરૂ કરવા દો	*tene kām juldee shuroŏ kurvā do*
He has full sympathy with me	તેને મારા તરફ પૂરી લાગણી છે	*tene mārā turuf pooree lāgnee che*
Come, let us take a walk in the garden	ચાલો, આપણે બગીચામાં ફરીએ	*chālo āpne bugeechā-mān furee-e*
I am sorry to say he is not a good man	મારે દિલગિરી સાથે કહેવું પડે છે કે તે સારો માણસ નથી	*māre dilgiree sāthe kuhevoŏn pudeche ke te sāro mānus nuthee*
Their friendship will not last long	તેમની દોસ્તી લાંબો વખત ટકશે નહિ	*temnee dostee lānbo vukhut tukshe nuhi*
I have made up	મારા નોકરને કહ્યો ...	*mārā nokurne*

English	Gujarati	Gujarati (romanized)
my mind to dismiss my servant	વાનો મે નિશ્ચય કર્યો છે	*kāḏhee moŏkvāno mein nish-chay kuryo c͟h*
He is a candidate for the vacant post	ખાલી જગોને માટે તે ઉમેદવાર છે	*k͟hālee jugone māṯe te ŏomedvār c͟he*
Leave off every bad habit	દરેક ખરાબ ટેવ છોડી દો	*durek k͟hurāb ṯev c͟hoḏee do*
Why are you afraid of that man?	તમે તે માણસથી શા માટે ડરો છો ?	*tume te māṇusthee shā māṯe ḏuro c͟ho?*
The climate of Bombay does not agree with me	મુંબઇનાં હવાપાણી મને માફક આવતાં નથી	*moŏnbui-nān huvā-pāṇee mune māfuk āvtān nuthee*
He did not answer my question.	તેણે મારા સવાલનો જવાબ આપ્યો નહિ	*teṇe mārā suvālno juvāb āpyo nuhi*
Light a candle or a lamp	મિણબત્તી અથવા ફાનસ સળગાવો	*miṇbuttee uthvā fānus suḷgāvo*
Do you know how to ride?	તમને ઘોડે બેસતાં આવડે છે ?	*tumne ghoḏe bestān āvḏe c͟he ?*
I am satisfied with his work	મને તેના કામથી સંતોષ છે	*mune tenā kāmthee suntos͟h c͟he*
This man was ill, but he is now well	આ માણસ માંદો હતો, પણ હવે તેને ઠીક છે	*ā māṇus māndo huto, puṇ huve tene ṯheek c͟he*
I went to the station to see him off	હું તેને વળાવવાને સ્ટેશને ગયો હતો	*hoŏn tene vuḷāv-vāne steshune guyo huto*
In India, wood is used as fuel	હિંદુસ્તાનમાં બળતણ તરીકે લાકડાં વપરાય છે	*hindoŏstān-mān buḷ-tuṇ turike lākḏān vuprāy c͟he*
Give my compliments to your father	તમારા બાપને મારા સલામ કહેજો	*tumārā bāpne mārā sulām kuhejo*

English	Gujarati	Gujarati (romanized)
Your good advice had no effect upon him	તમારી સારી સલાહની તેના ઉપર કાંઇ અસર થઇ નહિ	*tumāree sāree sulāhnee tenā oopur kān-i usur thu-i nuhi*
I have received no reply to my petition	મારી અરજીનો કાંઇ જવાબ મળ્યો નથી	*māree urjeeno kān-i juvāb muḷyo nuthee*
A flock of sheep were grazing in the field	ઘેટાંનું ટોળું ખેતરમાં ચરતું હતું	*ghetān-noon toḷoon kheturmān churtoon hutoon*
I am not esponsible for his mistakes	તેની ભૂલોને માટે હું જવાબદાર નથી	*tenee bhoolone māte hoon juvābdār nuthee*
I rescued him from drowning	મેં તેને ડૂબતો બચાવ્યો	*men tene ḍoobto buchāvyo*
I do not approve of his conduct	તેની વર્તણુક મને પસંદ નથી	*tenee vurtṇook mune pusund nuthee*
This boy is afraid of a dog	આ છોકરો કૂતરાથી ડરે છે	*ā chokro kootrāthee ḍure che*
He ran away on seeing a tiger	વાઘ જોઇને તે નાસી ગયો	*vāgh jo-i-ne te nāsee guyo*
He made off with the money	પૈસા લઇને તે ભાગી ગયો	*paisā lu-i-ne te bhāgee guyo*
They quarrelled among themselves	તેઓ અંદર અંદર લડી મૂઆ	*teo undur undur luḍee mooā*
It is twelve by my watch	મારા ઘડિયાળમાં બાર વાગ્યા છે	*mārā ghuḍiyāḷmān bār vāgyā che*
Why do you not act according to your promise ?	તમે તમારા વચન પ્રમાણે શા માટે વર્તતા નથી ?	*tume tumārā vuchun prumāṇe shāmāte vurt-tā nuthee*
I have no interest in this matter	આ બાબતમાં મારૂં કાંઇ હિત નથી	*ā bābutmān māroon kān-i hit nuthee*

English	Gujarati	Gujarati (romanized)
Your remarks are much too severe	તમારી ટીકા ઘણીજ સખત છે	*tumāree teek ghuneej sukhut che*
My house is too small for my family	મારૂં ઘર મારા કુટુંબ માટે ઘણુંજ નાનું છે	*māroon ghur mārā kootoonb māte ghunoonj nānoon che*
I saw twenty rupees lying on your table	મેં તમારા મેજ ઉપર વીસ રૂપિયા પડેલા જોયા હતા	*min tumārā mej oopur vees roopiyā pudelā joyā hutā*
Fetch me a saw from a carpenter	સુતારને ત્યાંથી કરવત લઇ આવો	*sootārne tyānthee kurvut lu-i āvo*
Tell me where the city gate is	ગામનો દરવાજો ક્યાં છે તે મને કહો	*gāmno durvājo kyān che te mune kuho*
Why do you look so pale and out of spirits ?	તમે આટલા બધા નિસ્તેજ અને ઉદાસ કેમ જણાઓ છો ?	*tume ātlā budhā nistej une oodās kem junā-o cho ?*
How do you account for the loss?	નુકસાનને માટે તમારો શું ખુલાસો છે ?	*nooksān-ne māte tumāro shoon khoolāso che ?*
I do not know how he came by this money	આ પૈસા તેની પાસે કેવી રીતે આવ્યા તે હું જાણતો નથી	*ā paisā tenee pāse kevee reete āvyā te hoon jānto nuthee*

Idiomatic Expressions.

Cut the matter short	ટુંકામાં પતાવો	*toonkāmān putāvo*
Never mind	કાંઇ ફિકર નહિ	*kān-i fikur nuhi*
Whither away so fast ?	આમ ઉતાવળા ક્યાં ચાલ્યા?	*ām ootāvulā kyān chālyā?*
That will do	બસ	*bus*
Do not be long	વાર લગાડશો નહિ	*vār lugādsho nuhi*

English	Gujarati	Gujarati (romanized)
Here it is	આ રહ્યું	*ā ruhyŏŏn*
It is all humbug	એ બધું ખોટું છે	*e budhŏŏn khotŏŏn che*
Do not waste your breath	બોલ બોલ કરો માં	*bol bol kuro mīn*
How are you getting on ?	કેમ ચાલે છે ?	*kem chāle che?*
I cannot help going	મારે ગયા વિના ચાલે તેમ નથી	*māre guyā vinā chāle tem nuthee*
He is in a good humour	તે આનંદમાં છે	*te ānunnd-mān che*
He is not in a good humour	તેનો મિજાજ ઠેકાણે નથી	*teno mijāj thekāne nuthee*
He made a mess of it	તેણે બધું બગાડયું	*tene budhŏŏn bugādyŏŏn*
It is very good on your part	આપની ઘણી મહેરબાની થઇ	*āpnee ghuneemuherbānee thu-i*
He is good for nothing	તે તદન નકામો છે	*te tudun nukāmo che*
Do not be silly	મૂર્ખ થાઓ માં	*moorkh thā-o mān*
Have patience	ધીરજ રાખો	*dheeruj rākho*
What do you mean?	શું કહેવા માગો છો ?	*shŏŏn kuhevā māg cho ?*
I nearly fell from the horse	હું ઘોડેથી પડતો પડતો બચ્યો	*hŏŏn ghodethee pudto pudto buchyo*
Will you do me a favour ?	મારા ઉપર એક મહેરબાની કરશો ?	*mārā ŏŏpur ek muherbānee kursho?*
I am very much obliged to you	આપનો મોટો ઉપકાર થયો	*āpno moto ŏŏpkār thuyo*
That cannot be	એમ હોય નહિ	*em hoy nuhi*
Take care	સંભાળજો; ખબરદાર	*sunbhāljo; khuburdār*

English	Gujarati	Gujarati (romanized
What a shame!	શરમની વાત છે !	*shurumnee vāt che!*
He is confined to bed	તે પથારીવશ છે	*te puthārcevush che*
He was deaf to my advice	તેણે મારી શિખામણમાની નહિ	*tene mree shikhā-mun mānee nuhi*
I have no faith in your story	હું તમારી વાત માનતો નથી	*hōōn t māree vāt m into nuthee*
He made a clean breast of it.	તેણે સાચે સાચી વાત કહી દીધી	*tene sāche sāchee vāt kuhee deedhee*
They are at daggers drawn	તેઓને બનતું નથી	*teone buntōōn nuthee*
You are a day after the fair	તમે જરા મોડા પહોંચ્યા	*tume jurā modā puhonchyā*
Walls have ears	આ વાત લઇ જાય	*vī vāt lu-i jā-y*
Ever and anon	કોઇ કોઇ વાર	*ko-i ko-i vār*
With open eyes	જાણી જોઇને	*jāne jo-i-ne*
To make faces	ચાળા પાડવા	*chālā pādvā*
I am in a fix	હું મુશ્કેલીમાં છું	*hōōn mōōshkeleemān chōōn*
It is a got up story	એ વાત જોડી કાઢેલી છે	*e vāt jodee kādhelee che*
He made good the loss	તેણે નુકસાની ભરી આપી	*tene nōōksānee bhuree āpee*
Lion's share	સૌથી મોટો ભાગ	*sowthee moto bhāg*
He lives from hand to mouth	તે માંડ માંડ પોતાનું પેટ ભરે છે	*te mānd mānd potā-nōōn pet bhure che*
He lays out money at interest	તે વ્યાજે પૈસા ધીરે છે	*te vyāje paisā dheere che*
He is a man of letters	તે વિદ્વાન છે	*te vidvān che*
To draw a long bow	મોટી મોટી વાતો કરવી	*motee motee vāto kurvee*

English	Gujarati	Gujarati (romanized)
It is all moonshine	એ બધું ખોટું છે	*e budhoon khotoon che*
He picked the lock	તેણે તાળું તોડયું	*tene tāloon todyoon*
He has poisoned your ears	તેણે તમારા કાન ભંભેર્યા છે	*tene tumārā kān bhunbherya che*
He drives a roaring trade	તેનો વેપાર ધમધોકાર ચાલે છે	*teno vepār dhum-dhokār chāle che*
To set up a shop	દુકાન માંડવી	*dookān mānḍvee*
I am short of funds	મારી પાસે પૈસા ખુટયા છે	*māree pāse paisā khootyā che*
He took off his coat	તેણે ડગલો ઉતાર્યો	*tene ḍuglo ootāryo*
To shed tears	આંસુ પાડવાં	*ānsoo pāḍvān*
To laugh in one's sleeve	મૂછમાં હસવું	*mooch-mān husvoon*
He has seen the ups and downs of life	તેણે જિંદગીનાં સુખ દુખ જોયાં છે	*tene jindgee-nān sookh dookh joyān che*

Travelling by Railway.

See Vocabulary page 27.

English	Gujarati	Gujarati (romanized)
Get every thing ready	તૈયારી કરો	*taiyāree kuro*
I shall go by the ten o'clock train	દસ વાગ્યાની ગાડીમાં હું જવાને છું	*dus vāgyā-nee gādee-mān hoon juvāno choon*
Order a carriage	ગાડી મંગાવો	*gādee mungāvo*
Is the luggage ready ?	સામાન તૈયાર છે ?	*sāmān taiyār che ?*
Put it on the carriage	ગાડીમાં રાખી દો	*gādee-mān rākhee do*
It is late; drive quickly to the station	મોડું થયું છે; સ્ટેશન તરફ જલદી હાંકો	*modoon thuyoon che; steshun turuf juldee hānko*

English	Gujarati	Gujarati (romanized)
I shall hardly catch the train	ટ્રેન માંડ મળશે	*tren mānḍ mulshe*
What is your fare?	ભાડું કેટલું આપું ?	*bhāḍoon ketloon āpoon*
Where is the booking office ?	ટિકેટ ઑફિસ કયાં છે ?	*tiket-ofis kyān che?*
A first class ticket to—	—ની પહેલા વર્ગની ટિકેટ આપો	*—nee puhelā vurg-ne tiket āpo*
What is the railway fare?	ટિકેટના કેટલા પૈસા આપું ?	*tiketnā ketlā pais āpoon?*
When does the train start ?	ગાડી કયારે ઉપડે છે ?	*gāḍee kyāre oopḍe che?*
In half an hour	અર્ધા કલાકમાં ઉપડશે	*urdhā kulākmān oopuḍshe*
When will it arrive at—?	—કયારે પહોંચશે ?	*—kyāre puhonchshe?*
Must I change any where ?	ગાડી કયાંઇ બદલવી પડશે?	*gāḍee kyān-i budulvee puḍshe?*
It stops at—for an hour	—સ્ટેશને એક કલાક રોકાશે	*—steshune ek kulāk rokāshe*
Where is dinner to be had ?	ખાણું કયાં મળશે ?	*khānoon kyān mulshe ?*
The luggage will go by goods train	સામાન માલગાડીમાં જશે	*sāmān mālgāḍee mān jushe*
What does it weigh?	વજન કેટલું છે ?	*vujun ketloon che ?*
What is the freight?	ભાડું શું પડશે ?	*bhāḍoon shoon puḍshe ?*
Put the luggage in the brake-van	સામાન બ્રેકમાં મૂકો	*sāmān brek-mān mooko*
Put the bedding and portmanteau in the carriage	પથારી અને પેટી ગાડીમાં મૂકો	*puthāree une petee gāḍee-mān mooko*

English	Gujarati	Gujarati (romanized)
Pay the porters	મજૂરને પૈસા આપી દો	*mujoorne paisā āpee do*

Breakfast, Tea, Dinner &c.

See Vocabulary page 22.

English	Gujarati	Gujarati (romanized)
Is breakfast ready?	નાસ્તો તૈયાર છે ?	*nāsto taiyār che ?*
Is the tea made?	ચા બનાવી ?	*chā buvāvee ?*
Bring a cup of tea	ચાનોં પ્યાલો લાવો	*chāno pyālo lāvo*
Will you take something with tea?	ચા સાથે કાંઇ લેશો ?	*chā sāthe kān-i lesho ?*
Yes, bring a piece of bread	હા, રોટલીનો કટકો લાવો	*hā. rotleeno kutko lāvo*
Bring me some fresh butter	મારે વાસ્તે થોડું તાજું માખણ લાવો	*māre vāste thodōōn tājōōn mākhun lāvo*
This cream is sour	આ મલાઇ ખાટી છે	*ā mulāi khātee ch*
I want sugar and milk	મારે ખાંડ અને દૂધ જોઇએ છે	*māre khānd un doodh joi-e che*
Are you hungry?	તમને ભુખ લાગી છે ?	*tumne bhookh lāgee che ?*
Are you thirsty ?	તમને તરસ લાગી છે?	*tumne turus lāgee che?*
Yes. I am very hungry	હા. મને મને બહુ ભૂખ લાગી છે	*hā. mune buhōō bhōōkh lāgee che*
These eggs are hard	આ ઇંડાં સખત છે	*ā indān sukhut che*
This egg is underdone	આ ઇંડું કાચું છે	*ā indōōn kāchōōn che*
Give me salt, pepper and mustard	મને મીઠું, મરી અને રાઇ આપો	*mune meethōōn, muree une ri-i āpo*
Bring a knife, fork and spoon	છરી, કાંટો અને ચમચો લાવો	*churee, kānto une chumcho lāvo*
Give me some more coffee	મને થોડી વધારે કાફી આપો	*mune thodee vudhāre kāfee āpo*

English	Gujarati	Gujarati (romanized)
Eight o'clock is our dinner time	અમારો જમવાનો વખત આઠ વાગ્યાનો છે	*umāro jumvāno vu-khut āth vāgyā-no che*
Come exactly at half-past seven	બરાબર સાડા સાત વાગ્યે આવજો	*burābur sādā sāt vāgye āvjo*
Help yourself	મરજી પડે તે લો	*murjee pude te lo*
Give him a glass of wine	તેને દારૂનો પ્યાલો આપો	*tene dāroo-no pyālo āpo*
Remove the dishes	રકાબીઓ લઇ જાઓ	*rukābee-o lu-i jā-o*
Serve the dinner	ખાણું પીરસો	*khānoon peerso*
We drank to the health of the Emperor	અમે શહેનશાહની સલામતી લેવડાવી	*ume shuhenshāh-nee sulāmutee levdāvee*

In Town.

English	Gujarati	Gujarati (romanized)
Where shall we go?	આપણે ક્યાં જઇશું ?	*āpne kyān ju-i-shoon ?*
Which is the way to—?	—જવાનો રસ્તો કયો ?	*—juvāno rusto kuyo ?*
Where does this road lead to ?	આ રસ્તો ક્યાં જાય છે ?	*ā rusto kyān jā-y che ?*
Go straight on	સીધા ચાલ્યા જાઓ	*seedhā chālyā jā-o*
Turn to the right	જમણી તરફ વળજો	*jumnee turuf vuljo*
Turn to the left	ડાબી તરફ વળજો	*dābee turuf vuljo*
Go to the other side of the road	રસ્તાની પેલી તરફ જાઓ	*rustā-nee polee turuf jā-o*
Is it far from here?	અહિંથી તે દૂર છે ?	*uhinthee te door che*
How far is it to—?	—અહિંથી કેટલું દૂર છે ?	*—uhinthee ketloon door che?*
About a mile	આશરે એક માઇલ	*āshre ek māil*
Where can I get a carriage to the post office ?	ટપાલ ઓફિસે જવા માટે ગાડી ક્યાં મળશે ?	*tupāl ofise juvā māte gādee kyān mulshe ?*

English	Gujarati	Gujarati (romanised)
Go quickly	જલદી જાઓ	*juldee jā-o*
Go slowly	ધીમેથી જાઓ	*dheem-thee jā-o*
Straight on	સીધા જાઓ	*seedhā jā-o*
Let us go	ચાલો	*chālo*
Show me the way	મને રસ્તો બતાવો	*mune rusto butāvo*
Keep to the left	ડાબી તરફ ચાલ્યા જાઓ	*ḍābee turuf chālyā jā-o*
Cross the road	સડક ઓળંગો	*suḍuk olungo*
What street is the shop in ?	તે દુકાન કઇ શેરીમાં છે?	*te dŏokān kuee sheree-mān ch̲e?*
Is this the way to the bazaar ?	બજારમાં જવાનો આ રસ્તો છે ?	*bujār-mān juvāno ā rusto ch̲e?*
Do you know Mr. F. ?	ફ. સાહેબને ઓળખો છો?	*F. sāheb-ne tume olk̲h̲o ch̲o?*
I do not know anyone of that name	એ નામના કોઇ શખ્સને હું ઓળખતો નથી	*e nāmnā koee shukhsne hŏon olk̲h̲uto nuthee*
He is a friend of mine	તે મારો મિત્ર છે	*te māro mitr ch̲e*
I know him very well	હું તેને સારી પેઠે ઓળખું છું	*hŏon tene sāree pethe olk̲h̲ŏon ch̲h̲ŏon*
Where are you going ?	તમે ક્યાં જાઓ છો ?	*tume kyān jā-o ch̲o?*
Where does he live ?	તે ક્યાં રહે છે ?	*te kyān ruhe ch̲e?*
Close by	નજીકમા	*nujeek-mān*
Can you direct me to his house ?	એમનું ઘર મને બતાવશો?	*emnŏon gh̲ur mune butāvsho?*
Here it is	આ રહ્યું	*ā ruhyŏon*
Is Mr.—at home?	—સાહેબ ઘેર છે ?	*—sāheb gh̲er ch̲e?*
He is not in	સાહેબ ઘેર નથી	*sāheb gh̲er nuthee*

Shopping.

See Vocabulary page 31.

English	Gujarati	Gujarati (romanized)
I want to buy some cotton (hides, rice, wheat)	મારે રૂ (ચામડાં, ચોખા, ઘઉં) ની ખરીદ કરવી છે	*māre rŏŏ (chāmḍāṅ chokhā, ghuŏŏṅ) nee khureed kurvee che*
Show some samples	નમૂના બતાવો	*numoonā butāvo*
What price ?	શો ભાવ છે ?	*sho bhāv che?*
How much a yard?	વારનું શું ?	*vār-nŏŏṅ shŏŏṅ?*
What is the width?	પનો કેટલો છે ?	*puno ketlo che?*
What is the length	લંબાઇ કેટલી છે ?	*lumbāi ketlee che ?*
It is very dear	બહુ મોંઘું છે	*buhŏŏ monghŏŏṅ che*
It is too much	બહુ વધારે છે	*buhŏŏ vudhāre che*
Have you anything cheaper ?	એથી સસ્તો માલ છે	*ethee susto māl che?*
I want this sort of cotton	આ જાતનું રૂ મારે જોઇએ છે	*ā jātnŏŏṅ rŏŏ māre joi-e che*
Measure ten yards	દસ વાર ભરો	*dus vār bhuro*
Show me another kind of cloth	બીજી જાતનું કાપડ બતાવો	*beejee jātnŏŏṅ kāpuḍ butāvo*
I prefer this	આ મને પસંદ છે	*ā mune pusund che*
I shall buy this one	મારે આ લેવું છે	*māre ā levŏŏṅ che*
I do not like it	મને તે પસંદ નથી	*mune te pusund nuthee*
What is your lowest price ?	ઓછામાં ઓછો શો ભાવ?	*ochā-māṅ ocho sho bhāv?*
Reduce your price	ભાવ ઓછો કરો	*bhāv ocho kuro*
I will not give so much for it	એનું એટલું બધું નહિ આપું	*enŏŏṅ etlŏŏṅ budhŏŏṅ nuhi āpŏŏṅ*
Will you take a cheque or cash?	હુંડી લેશો કે રોકડા રૂપિયા?	*hŏŏṅḍee lesho ke rokḍā rŏŏpiyā?*

English	Gujarati	Gujarati (romanized)
A demand bill will do	તરતની મુદતની હુંડીચાલશે	*turutnee moŏdut-nee hoŏntee chālshe*
Count the money	રૂપિયા ગણી લો	*roŏpiyā gunee lo*
Write out a receipt	પહોંચ લખી આપો	*puhoinch lukhee āpo*
Sign the receipt	પહોંચ ઉપર સહી કરો	*puhoinch oŏpur suhee kuro*
Your account is wrong	તમારો હિસાબ બરાબર નથી	*tumāro hisāb burābur nuthee*
Have you any good cotton?	તમારી પાસે સારૂં રૂ છે ?	*tumāree pāse sāroŏn roŏ che?*
This cotton is very inferior	આ રૂ બહુ હલકું છે	*ā roŏ buhoŏ hulkoŏn che*
The goods are damaged	માલ નુકસાનીવાળો છે	*māl noŏksānee-vālo che*
Give me an invoice	મને ભરતીઉં આપો	*mune bhurutiyoŏn āpo*
The goods do not correspond with the invoice	ભરતિયા પ્રમાણે માલ મળતો નથી	*bhurutiyā prumāne māl multo nuthee*
Get the goods insured	માલનો વીમો ઉતરાવો	*mālno veemo oŏtrāvo*
What is the rate of exchange to-day ?	આજ હુંડીનો શો ભાવછે?	*āj hoŏndee-no sho bhāv che?*
How much will you take for that?	તમે એનું શું લેશો ?	*tume enoŏn shoŏn lesho?*
What discount will you allow ?	વળતર શું આપશો ?	*vultur shoŏn āpsho?*
At cost price	પડતર ભાવે	*pudtur bhāve*
Bring your bill and I will settle it	હિસાબ લાવો એટલે ચુકતો કરી આપું	*hisāb lāvo etle choŏkto kuree āpoŏn*

English	Gujrati	Gujarati (romanized)
A detailed account	વિગતવાર હિસાબ	*vigutvār hisāb*
I shall pay the balance tomorrow	બાકી રૂપિયા કાલે આપીશ	*bākee rŏŏpiyā kāle āpeesh*
The market is dull	બજાર નરમ છે	*bujār nurum che*
The market is brisk	બજાર તેજ છે	*bujār tej che*
The price has risen	ભાવ વધ્યા છે	*bhāv vudhyā che*
The price has gone down	ભાવ ઘટયા છે	*bhāv ghutyā che*
Wholesale dealers	જથાબંધ વેચનાર	*juthā-bundh vechnār*
Retail sellers	છુટક વેચનાર	*chŏŏtuk vechnār*
Telegraph this afternoon	આજ બપોર પછી તાર કરજો	*āj bupor puchee tār kurjo*
There is a great demand for wheat	ઘઉંની બહુ ઘરાકી છે	*ghu-ŏŏn-nee buhŏŏ ghurākee che*
Account of sales and purchases	વેચાણ અને ખરીદનો હિસાબ	*vechāṇ une khureed-no hisāb*
How many pieces in a bale ?	એક ગાંસડીમાં કેટલા તાકા?	*ek gānsdee-mān ketlā takā?*
How is the market for those goods?	એ માલનો બજાર કેવો છે?	*e mālno bujār kevo che?*
Buy if possible	બની શકે તો ખરીદ કરો	*bunee shuke to khureed kuro*
What amount have you to sell ?	તમારે કેટલો માલ વેચવો છે?	*tumāre ketlo māl vechvo che?*
What profit do you want ?	કેટલો નફો લેશો ?	*ketlo nufo lesho?*
He has become bankrupt	તેણે દિવાળું કાઢયું છે	*tene divāḷŏŏn kādhyŏŏn che*
His business is going on well	તેનો વેપાર સારો ચાલે છે	*teno vepār sāro chāle che*

Correspondence.

English	Gujarati	Gujarati (romanized)
I must write a letter	મારે એક કાગળ લખવાનોછે	māre ek kāguḷ lukhvāno che
I want some paper	મારે કોરા કાગળ જોઇએ છે	māre korā kāguḷ jo-i-e che
Have you any?	તમારી પાસે છે ?	tumāree pāse che?
Will you give me some ?	મને થોડાક કાગળ આપશો?	mune thoḍāk kāguḷ āpsho?
Lend me a sheet	મને એક તા ઉછીનો આપો	mune ek tā ŏŏcheno āpo
This pen is bad	આ ટાંક ખરાબ છે	ā tānk khurāb che
Have you another?	તમારી પાસે બીજી છે ?	tumāree pāse beejee che?
Is your letter for the post ?	તમારો કાગળ ટપાલમાં નાખવાનો છે ?	tumāro kāguḷ tupāl mān nākhvāno che?
A postage stamp	ટપાલની ટિકેટ	tupālnee tiket
What is the day of the month ?	આજ તારીખ કઇ થઇ ?	āj tārekh ku-i thui?
To-day is the first	આજ પહેલી તારીખ થઇ	āj puhelee tāreekh thu-i
What is the day of the week ?	આજ શો વાર થયો ?	āj sho vār thuyo?
To-day is Monday	આજ સોમવાર થયો	āj som-vār thuyo
Close the envelope	કવર બંધ કરો	kuvur bundh kuro
Seal your letter	કાગળને લાખથી મહોરકરો	kāguḷne lākh-thee muhor kuro
There is no wax	લાખ નથી	lākh nuthee
Send a reply	જવાબ લખો	juvāb lukho
Take this letter to the post	આ કાગળ ટપાલે લઇજાઓ	ā kāguḷ tupāle lu-i jā-o
Pay the postage	ટિકેટના પૈસા આપી દેજો	tiketnā paisā āpee dejo

To Domestic Servants

English	Gujarati	Gujarati (romanized)
Send the groom here	ઘોડાવાળાને અહિં મોકલો	*ghodwālāne uhin moklo*
Do you understand what I say ?	હું કહું છુ તે તમે સમજો છો?	*hoŏn kuhoŏn choŏn te tume sumjo cho?*
How much grain do you give to the horse every day ?	ઘોડાને દરરોજ કેટલા ચણા આપો છો ?	*ghodāne dur-roj ketlā chunā āpo cho ?*
Have you groomed the horse this morning ?	ઘોડાને આજ સવારે માલિશ કર્યો છે ?	*ghodāne āj suvāre mālish kuryo che?*
Saddle the pony and bring it here	ટટ્ટુ ઉપર જીન નાખો અને અહિં લાવો	*tuttoŏ oŏpur jeen nākho une uhin lāvo*
Take the bridle to the shoemaker and get it mended.	લગામ મોચી પાસે લઇ જાઓ અને તે દુરસ્ત કરાવી લાવો	*lugām mochee pāse lu-i jāo une te doŏrust kurāvee lāvo*
Call the washerman	ધોબીને બોલાવો	*dhobeene bolāvo*
You have not washed the clothes well this time	આ વખતે કપડાં બરાબર ધોયાં નથી	*ā vukhte tume kupdan burābur dhoyān nuthee*
See, how badly this is done ?	જુઓ, આ કેવું ખરાબ બનાવ્યું છે ?	*joŏ-o ā kevoŏn khurāb bunāvyoŏn che?*
The shirts are too limp	ખમીસ બહુ નરમ છે	*khumees buhoŏ nurum che*
You have not put enough starch in them	તેમાં જોઇએ તેટલી કાંજી નાખી નથી	*temān joi-e tetlee kānjee nākhee nuthee*

English	Gujarati	Gujarati (romanized)
You have not ironed them well	બરાબર ઇસ્ત્રી પણ કરી નથી	*burābur istree puṇ kuree nuthee*
Where are the two sheets I gave you to wash ?	બે ચાદર ધોવા આપી હતી તે ક્યાં છે ?	*be chādur dhovā āpee hutee te kyān che ?*
You have torn my handkerchief	મારો રૂમાલ તમે ફાડી નાખ્યો છે	*māro roomāl tume fāḍee nākhyo che?*
This pair of socks is not mine	આ મોજાની જોડી મારી નથી	*ā mojānee joḍee māree nuthee*
Take it back and bring me mine	તે પાછી લઇ જાઓ અને મારી લઇ આવો	*te pāchee lui jāo une māree lui āvo*
I miss a collar	મારો કોલર ક્યાં છે ?	*māro kolur kyān che ?*
This coat is scorched	આ ડગલો દાઝી ગયો છે	*ā ḍuglo dājhee guyo che*
You put too much blue in my linen	મારાં કપડાંમાં બહુ ગળી નાંખો છો	*mārān kupḍān-mān buhoo guḷe nākho cho*
Have you your bill ?	તમારો હિસાબ લાવ્યા છો?	*tumāro hisāb lāvyā cho ?*
I will pay you tomorrow	કાલે પૈસા આપીશ	*kāle puisā āpeesh*
Return these clothes on Sunday next	આવતા રવિવારે આ કપડાં ધોઇને લાવજો	*āvtā ruvi-vāre ā kupḍān dhoin lāvjo*
Where is the peon?	પટાવાળો ક્યાં છે ?	*putāvāḷo kyān che?*
Take this note to Mr. Smith	આ ચિઠી સ્મિથ સાહેબ પાસે લઇ જાઓ	*ā chiṭhee Smith sāheb pāse lu-i jāo*
If he is not at home, wait till he comes back	સાહેબ ઘેર ન હોય તો પાછા આવે ત્યાંસુધી રાહ જોજો	*sāheb gher nu hoy to pāchā āve tyān soodhee rāh jojo*

English	Gujarati	Gujarati (romanized)
Bring an answer	જવાબ લઇને આવજો	*juvāb lu-ine āvjo*
Tell the clerk to copy this letter	આ કાગળની નકલ કરવાનું કારકુનને કહો	*ā kāguḷnee nukul kurvānŏŏn kārkŏŏn-ne kuho*
Gum this envelope and seal it	આ કવરને ગુંદર લગાડો અને તેને મહોર કરો	*ā kuvurne gŏŏndur lugāḍo une tene muhor kuro*
Then take it to the Post Office	પછી તે ટપાલ ઓફિસે લઇ જાઓ	*puchee te ṭupāl ofise lu-i jāo*
Take these books to the library and bring some new ones	આ ચોપડીઓ પુસ્તકશાળામાં લઇ જાઓ અને બીજી નવી લઇ આવો	*ā chopḍee-o pŏŏstukshāḷā mān lu-i jāo une beejee nuvee lu-i āvo*
Hold your tongue	ચુપ રહો	*chŏŏp ruho*
I do not want to hear you	મારે તમારૂં સાંભળવું નથી	*māre tumārŏŏn sānbhuḷvŏŏn nuthee*
I shall fine you	હું તમારો દંડ કરીશ	*hŏŏn tumāro dunḍ kureesh*
I shall dismiss you	હું તમને કાઢી મુકીશ	*hŏŏn tumne kāḍhee mŏŏkeesh*
Are you not ashamed of yourself?	તમને શરમ નથી લાગતી?	*tumne shurum nuthee lāgtee?*
Go away; do not show me your face again	ચાલ્યા જાઓ, તમારૂં મ્હોં મને ફરીથી બતાવશો નહિ	*chālyā jā-o tumārŏŏn mhon mune furee-thee butāvsho nuhi*
Well done. I am very pleased with you	શાબાશ. હું તમારા ઉપર બહુ ખુશી થયો છું	*shābāsh. hŏŏn tumārā ŏŏpur buhŏŏ khŏŏshee thuyo chŏŏn*

English	Gujarati	Gujarati (romanized)
Tell the coachman to take the carriage to the station	ગાડીવાળાને કહો કે ગાડી સ્ટેશને લઇ જાય	*gādeevāḷā-ne kuho ke gādee steshune lu-i jay*
Tell the cook there are two guests to dine with me today	રસોયાને કહો કે આજે બે મહેમાન મારી સાથે જમવાના છે	*rusoyāne kuho ke āje be muhemān māree sāthe jumvānā che*

Fishing.

See Vocabulary page 37.

English	Gujarati	Gujarati (romanized)
Is there any fishing to be had near here ?	આટલામા માછલાં મારવાનું કોઇ ઠેકાણું છે ?	*ātlāmān māchlān mārvānoon ko-i thekāṇoon che ?*
Must I first obtain permission to fish?	માછલાં મારવાની પરવાનગી પહેલેથી લેવી પડશે?	*māchlān mārvānee purvāngee puhele-thee levee pudshe ?*
Can I have a boat and man ?	એક હોડી અને આદમી મળી શકશે ?	*ek hodee une ādmee muḷee shukshe?*
What do you charge for the hour ?	કલાકનું તમે શું લેશો ?	*kulāk-noōn tume shoōn lesho?*
Are you an experienced fisherman ?	તમે અનુભવી મચ્છીમાર છો?	*tume unoōbhuvee muchcheemār cho?*
Can I depend on you ?	તમારા ભરોસે રહું ?	*tumārā bhurose ruhoōn?*
Will you bring bait ?	તમે ગલ લાવશો ?	*tume gul lāvsho ?*
Have you brought some bait ?	તમે ગલ લાવ્યા છો ?	*tume gul lāvyā cho?*
Give me a hook	મને આંકડી આપો	*mune ānkdee āpo*

English	Gujarati	Gujarati (romanized)
The weather is unfavourable	હવા અનુકુળ નથી	*huvā unoŏkoŏḷ nuthee*
The oars	હલેસાં	*hulesān*
Row gently	હોડી ધીમી ચલાવો	*hoḍee dheemee chulāvo*
This is a good place	આ સારી જગ્યા છે	*ā sāree jugyā che*
Stop rowing	હલેસાં બંધ રાખો	*hulesān bundh rākho*
Don't make a noise	અવાજ કરો મા	*uvāj kuro mān*
Make haste	જલદી કરો	*juldee kuro*
How much does this fish weigh?	આ માછલીનું વજન કેટલું હશે ?	*ā māchlee-noŏn vujun ketloŏn hushe?*
Will you weigh it?	તમે તોળી જોશો ?	*tume toḷee josho?*
The fishing is good here	માછલાં મારવાની આ સારી જગ્યા છે	*māchlān mārvānee ā sāree jugyā che?*
Fishing tackle	માછલાં મારવાનો સામાન	*māchlān mārvāno sāmān*
The line	દોરી	*doree*
Fishing net	જાળ	*jāḷ*

Shooting.

See Vocabulary page 37.

English	Gujarati	Gujarati (romanized)
Have I to obtain permission to shoot here ?	મારે અહિં શિકારકરવાની પરવાનગી લેવી પડશે ?	*māre uhin shikār kurvānee purvāngee levee pudshe?*
To whom must I apply ?	કોની પરવાનગી લેવી જોઇએ ?	*konee purvāngee levee jo-i-e?*
What kind of game can I get here ?	અહિં કેવી જાતનો શિકાર મળી શકશે ?	*uhin kevee jātno shikār muḷee shukshe?*

English	Gujarati	Gujarati (romanized)
Can I obtain the exclusive right over the shooting?	મને એકલાને શિકાર કરવાનો હક મળી શકશે ?	*mune eklāne shikār kurvāno huk muḷee shuksh ?*
What rent must I pay ?	ભાડું શું આપવું પડશે?	*bhāḍoon shoon āp-voon puḍshe?*
Can I get one or two experienced men to go out shooting with me?	મારી સાથે શિકારે જવા માટે એક બે હોશિયાર આદમી મળી શકશે ?	*māree sāthe shikāre juvā māṭe ek be hoshiyār ādmee muḷee shukshe?*
How much must I pay each of them per day ?	દરેકને દરરોજના કેટલા પૈસા આપવા પડશે ?	*durekne dur-rojnā ketlā paisā āpvā puḍshe?*
How many dogs can you let me have ?	તમે મને કેટલા કુતરા આપી શકશો ?	*tume mune ketlā kootrā āpee shuk-sho?*
Are the dogs properly trained ?	કુતરા બરાબર કેળવાએલા છે ?	*kootrā burābur keḷ-vāyelā che?*
Keep the dogs back	કુતરાને પાછળ રાખો	*kootrāne pāchhuḷ rā-kho*
Load my gun	મારી બંદૂક ભરો	*māree bundook bhuro*
Carry my gun	મારી બંદૂક લઇ ચાલો	*māree bundook lu-i chālo*
Give me some cartridges	મને થોડાં કાર્તુસ આપો	*mune thoḍān kār-toos āpo*
Do not fire	બંદૂક ફોડોમાં	*bundook foḍo mān*
Take good aim	બરાબર નિશાન તાકો	*burābur nishān tāko*
Let me have a shot with your gun	તમારી બંદૂકથી મને ગોળી મારવા દો	*tumāree bundook-thee mune goḷee mārvā do*
Gunpowder; barrel	દારૂ; નળી	*dāroo; nuḷee*
To cock a gun	ઘોડો ચડાવવો	*ghoḍo chuḍāv-vo*

Time and Weather.

See Vocabulary page 14.

English	Gujarati	Gujarati (romanized)
What o'clock is it?	કેટલા વાગ્યા છે ?	*ketlī vāgyā che ?*
It is half past seven	સાડા સાત વાગ્યા છે	*sāḍā sāt vāgyā che*
It is a quarter past nine	સવા નવ વાગ્યા છે	*suvā nuv vāgyā che*
It is ten minutes to one	એકમા દસ કમ છે	*ekmān dus kum che*
It is five minutes past two	બે ઉપર પાંચ મિનિટ થઇ છે	*be oŏpur pānch minit thu-i che*
The clock has struck three	ઘડિયાળમાં ત્રણ વાગ્યા છે	*ghuḍiyāḷmān truṇ vāgyā che*
Come within half an hour	અરધા કલાકમાં આવજે	*urdhā kulākmān āvjo*
It would take me three quarters of an hour	મને પોણો કલાક લાગશે	*mune poṇo kulāk lāgshe*
He came late by two hours	તે બે કલાક મોડો આવ્યો	*te be kulāk moḍo āvyo*
Why does he come late every day?	તે દરરોજ મોડે શામાટે આવે છે ?	*te dur-roj moḍo shā māte āve che?*
Wind the clock and set the hands right	ઘડિયાળને ચાવી આપો અને કાંટા બરાબર મુકો	*ghuḍiyāḷne chāvee āpo une kāntā burābur mooko*
The English Mail arrives every Friday	વિલાયતનો મેલ દર શુક્રવારે આવે છે	*vilāyutno mel dur shookr-vāre āve che*
I had been to his house yesterday	કાલે હું તેને ઘેર ગયો હતો	*kāle hoon tene gher guyo huto*
I have no time today	આજે મને વખત નથી	*āje mune vukhut nuthee*

English	Gujarati	Gujarati (romanized)
Come tomorrow morning	કાલ સવારે આવજો	*kāl suvāre āvjo*
I shall write to him the day after tomorrow	હું તેને પરમ દિવસ કાગળ લખીશ	*hoon tene purum divus kāguḷ lukheesh*
I had guests the day before yesterday	પરમ દિવસ મારે ત્યાં મહેમાન હતા	*purum divus māre tyān muhemān hutā*
It is a fine morning	સવાર બહુ સુંદર છે	*suvār buhoo soondur che*
It is cloudy today	આજે વાદળાં છે	*āje vādḷān ch*
It was very hot yesterday afternoon	કાલ બપોરે ગરમી સખત હતી	*kāl bupore gurmee sukhut hutee*
It was very cold last night	ગઈ રાતે ઠંડી બહુ હતી	*gu-i rāte thundee buhoo hutee*
The rainy season this year was all that could be desired	આ વર્ષે ચોમાસું જોઈએ તેવું હતું	*ā vurshe chomāsoon jo-i-e tevoon hutoon*
It is very windy	પવન ઘણો છે	*puvun ghuṇo che*
It is very dusty	ધૂળ બહુ ઊડે છે	*dhooḷ buhoo oode che*
It is very close	ઉકળાટ ઘણો છે	*ookḷāt ghuṇo che*

V Exercises for Translation.

(A) Translation into English.

I.

કાગડો, a crow *m.*
બગલો, a crane *m.*
અદેખાઇ, envy *f.*
પાંખો, wings *f. p.*
દુબળો, feeble *d.*
અંતે, at last
ન્હાવું, to bathe

એક કાગડાને બગલાની ધોળી પાંખો જોઇને અદેખાઇ આવી. તેણે ધાર્યું કે તે હમેશાં નદી કાંઠે રહે છે અને પાણીમાં ન્હાય છે, તેથી તેની પાંખો ધોળી થઇ હશે. પછી તે નદી કાંઠે રહેવા ગયો, અને રોજ સવારે પાંખો ઘસીને સાફ કરવા લાગ્યો; પણ તે ધોળી થઇ નહિ. અંતે ખોરાક ન મળવાથી તે દુબળો થઇને મરી ગયો.

II.

સેવા, service *f.*
ઘા, wound *m.*
પેરણું, shirt *n.*
ડાઘ, scars *m. p.*
આગળનો ભાગ, front *m*
જોવું, to see; to consider
ઉતારવું, to take off
મંજુર કરવું, to grant

એક સિપાઇને પોતાના દેશની સેવા બજાવતાં ઘણા ઘા વાગેલા હતા. તેણે મદદને માટે રાજાને અરજ કરી. રાજાએ કહ્યું કે જોઇશું. સિપાઇએ પોતાનું પેરણું ઉતાર્યું અને ઘણા ઘાના ડાઘ બતાવીને કહ્યું કે સાહેબ, હમણાંજ જોઇ લો. રાજા જોઇને ખુશી થયો કે તેના બધા ઘા આગળના ભાગમાં હતા. તેણે તરતજ તેની અરજ મંજૂર કરી.

III.

પાડોશી, a neighbour *m.*
ઉંદરિયું, a mouse-trap *n.*
સંખ્યાબંધ, a number of
ફેલાઇ ગયા, spread
ચોતરફ, all over
તળીએથી, from the bottom
ચિઠી, a note *f.*
ભેટ, a present *f.*
સ્વીકારવું, to accept

એક માણસની વહાલી બિલાડીને તેના પાડોશીએ મારી નાખી. પેલા માણસને એ વાતની ખબર પડી એટલે તેણે બજારમાંથી એક ઉંદરિયું વેચાતું લીધું, અને તેમાં થોડાક જીવતા ઉંદર પકડયા. પછી તે એક પેટીમાં મૂકીને ને પેલા પાડોશીના ઘેર મોકલી. તેણે પેટી ઉઘાડી કે તરતજ સંખ્યાબંધ ઉંદર બહાર કૂદી પડયા, અને ઘરમાં ચોતરફ ફેલાઇ ગયા. પેટીના તળીએથી

એક ચિઠી મળી તેમાં લખ્યું હતું કે તમે મારી બિલાડી મારી ન ખી, તેથી આ સાથે થોડા ઉંદર ભેટ મોકલું છું તે સ્વીકારશો.

IV.

રાજ મહેલ, a royal palace *m.* લૂટારા, robbers *m. p.*
સલામતી, safety *f.* સગો, a relative *m.*
પાછળ પડવું, to go in pursuit ગુસ્સો ચઢવો, to be angry.

એક વખત નેપોલિયન ઇજિપ્તના રાજ મહેલમાં બેઠો હતો, એવામાં ખબર આવ્યા કે લૂટારા એક ભરવાડને મારીને તેના ઘેટાં હાંકી ગયા છે. નેપોલિયને તરતજ હુકમ કર્યો કે લશ્કર લઇને લૂટારાની પછાડી પડો અને તેમને પકડી લાવો. એ વખતે એક આરબ શેખ ત્યાં બેઠો હતો તે બોલ્યો કે આ ગરીબ ભરવાડ આપનો સગો થતો હતો કે આપને આટલો બધો ગુસ્સો ચઢ્યો ? નેપોલિયને જવાબ આપ્યો કે સગાં કરતાં પણ એ વધારે હતો, કારણકે ખુદાએ મને તેની સલામતી સોંપી હતી.

V.

છબી, a portrait *f.* ટોળું, a flock *n.*
લીન, intent દરકાર, care *f.*
નવાઇ લાગી, was surprised

એક વખત મહારાણી વિક્ટોરિયા રસ્તા વચ્ચે ઉભાં ઉભાં બાલમોરલ મહેલની છબી ચિતરતાં હતાં. એવામાં એક ભરવાડ ઘેટાંનું ટોળું લઇને એ રસ્તેથી નીકળ્યો. તેણે બુમ પાડી કે, ઓ ડોસી, રસ્તા વચ્ચે શામાટે ઉભી છે ? દૂર ખસી જા. મહારાણી પોતાના કામમાં એટલાં બધાં લીન થઇ ગયાં હતાં કે તેમણે તે સાંભળ્યું નહિ. પણ તેમનો એક નોકર પેલા ભરવાડ પાસે દોડી ગયો અને બોલ્યો કે એ કોણ છે તે તું જાણે છે ? ભરવાડે જવાબ આપ્યો કે હું જાણતો એ નથી અને મને જાણવાની દરકાર પણ નથી. પેલા નોકરે કહ્યું કે એ મહારાણી છે. એ સાંભળીને પેલા ભરવાડને નવાઇ લાગી અને તે બોલ્યો કે ત્યારે લોકો ઓળખી શકે એવાં કપડાં તે શા માટે પહેરતાં નથી ?

(B) Translation into Gujarati.

I.

Tank, તળાવ *n.* fun, ગમત *f.*
frogs, દેડકાં *n. p.* hurt, ઇજા કરવી
please, મહેરબાની કરીને but, ફક્ત
true, સાચુ consider, વિચાર કરો

Some boys were playing beside a tank and were

throwing stones into it for fun. The tank was full of frogs, and when the boys threw in stones, they hurt the poor frogs. Then one of the frogs put his head out of the water and said, " Please, do not throw stones at us." "We are but at play," said one of the boys. "True," said the frog " but the stones you throw hurt us. Consider, what is play to you is death to us."

II.

Oath, પ્રતિજ્ઞા *f.* — swore, પ્રતિજ્ઞા કરી કે
hung, લટકાવી — neck, ગરદન *f.*
proclaimed, જાહેર કર્યું કે — separately, જુદા જુદા
collar, ગળપટો *m.* — pleasant, ઠીક; મજેનું
had not been, ન હોત — it would have been, થાત

An Arab lost a camel. He swore, "If I find it, I shall sell it for one rupee." When he found it, he became sorry for his oath. He, then, hung a cat round the neck of the camel, and proclaimed, "I will sell the camel for one rupee and the cat for one hundred rupees, but I will not sell them separately." A man came there and said, "If there had been no collar on the neck of the camel, how very pleasant it would have been!"

III.

fisher, મચ્છીમાર *m.* — fish, માછલી *f.*
creature, પ્રાણી *n.* — use, લાભ *m.*
to grow, મોટી થવા — sure, ખાતરી
to let, જવા દેવું — to doubt, શક રહેવો
ever, કદિ — basket, ટોપલી *f.*
frying-pan, કડાઇ *f.*

A fisher had caught a very little fish. The poor creature said, " What is the use of catching me? Give me time to grow. Throw me back into the river and catch me when I am bigger." The fisher answered, " I am sure of you this time, but if I let you into the water again, I doubt if I may ever see you more. I will put you into my basket and you shall go into the frying-pan this evening."

IV.

closes, બંધ થાય છે	at ball, દડે
forget, ભૂલી જવું	everything, બધું,
was deceived, છેતરાઇ ગઇ	at all, મુદ્દલ
had been kept in, રોકયો હતો	lie, જુઠું *n.*
of course, અલબત્ત	else, બીજું

One day a mother said to her son, "It is six o'clock, and your school closes at four; where have you been?" "O mother," said Ned, " when we play at ball, we forget everything else." The boy's mother was deceived. From Ned's answer she thought that he had been playing. But he had not be n playing at all. He had been kept in by his teacher, because he had no learned his lesson. He did not like to tell his mother that.

"I did not tell a lie." said Ned to himself. What do you think ? Did Ned tell a lie, or did he not ? I am sure you will say, "Of course, he did."

V.

It seemed that એમ જણાયું કે

offer, અર્પણ કરવુ	precious, કીમતી
pray, પ્રાર્થના કરવી	perhaps, કદાચ
to spare, બચાવવું	life, જિંદગી
round, ફરતો; આસપાસ	bed, પથારી
instead, ને બદલે	got better, સાજો થયો

Babar did not live long in India. His son Humayun fell ill and it seemed that he would die. Some one said to Babar, "If you offer to God the most precious thing you have and pray to Him, perhaps He will spare the life of your son." On hearing this, Babar walked three times round his son's bed and prayed that God would spare his son's life and take his own instead. It seemed as if God had heard his prayer, for, from that time, Humayun got better while Babar grew weaker and at last he died.

VI. Money and Weights.

Money.

Gold.	1 sovereign	=	about 15 rupees	
				s. d.
Silver,	1 rupee	=	about	1—4
Silver,	$\frac{1}{2}$ rupee (*urdho*)	=	about	0 8
Silver,	$\frac{1}{4}$ rupee (*pavlee*)	=	about	0—4
Nickel,	$\frac{1}{8}$ rupee (*be ānee*)	=	about	0—2
Nickel,	$\frac{1}{16}$ rupee (*ek ānee*)	=	about	0—1
Copper,	$\frac{1}{32}$ rupee (*dhuboo*)	=	about	0—$\frac{1}{2}$
Copper,	$\frac{1}{64}$ rupee (*paiso*)	=	about	0—$\frac{1}{4}$
Copper,	$\frac{1}{192}$ rupee (*pie*)	=	about	0—$\frac{1}{12}$

Note—As a rule £ 1 (sterling) = 15 rupees; but these equivalents are subject to the fluctuations in exchange.

Weights

Gold and Silver.

3 *rutee*	= 1 *vāl*
16 *vāl*	= 1 *gudiāṇo*
2 *gudiāṇā* or 32 *vāl*	= 1 *tolā* (1 rupee-weight)
1 lb. av.	= $38\frac{4}{7}$ rupee-weight
1 lb. troy	= 32 rupee-weight
180 troy grain	= 1 rupee-weight

Other weights.

$2\frac{1}{2}$ rupee-weight	= 1 *udhol*	40 Ser	= 1 *maund*
5 rupee-weight	= 1 *nuv-ṭānk*	5 maund	= 1 *kothlī*
10 rupee-weight	= 1 *pā-ser*	16 maund	= 1 *kulsee*
20 rupee-weight	= 1 *urdho-ser*	20 maund	= 1 *khaṇḍee*
40 rupee-weight	= 1 *ser*		

Note:—Sers differ in different places. In Surat one Ser = 37 rupee-weight; in other places of Gujarat one Ser = 40 rupee-weight. In Bengal, the Deccan and the Punjab, one Ser = 80 rupee-weight. In Bombay city the weight of Ser differs with different commodities from 28 rupee-weight to 56.